A blinding white light appea
years ago in my darkest hou..., ...
write a book along with the title…

Out of the Dark
by
SIMON E LEE

BEATING DEPRESSION NATURALLY

Including a 12 day re-programming section that got
me out of depression. This book is not for anyone
with a perfect life.

Published by Simon E Lee

Copyright © Simon E. Lee 2016

First Edition

ISBN 978-0-9955311-0-9

To Avidai

This book is dedicated to my mother in Heaven
for her love and guidance

May my book have a positive difference in your life!

Lots of Love

Lmi

Acknowledgements

To my son for being my friend and the unconditional love we share for each other

To all my 6 sisters for putting up with me over the years

Thanks to Chris for his help with the book

To my client and dear friend Karren many thanks for help with editing the book

To my good friend Spiros for always being there

A special thank you to Connie in America for inspiring me to finish this book

To my daughter in law for her kindness and support

Thanks to Joy for caring and all of her wonderful therapies

Many thanks to Audrey and Chris for their love and kindness

A special thank you to Jayne Wallace and Liz Dean, renown Physic's working within Selfridges, London, and authors in their own right, for their kind help and guidance with this book.

Thanks to Jenny, my reflexologist, for being a guiding light.

And to all my good friends for their support

God bless you all.

Simon

Testimonials

What an inspirational book, I feel it will help us all to understand our spiritual path. It is well written and personally would highly recommend it.

Jayne Wallace
Psychic Sisters
Selfridges, London

Very informative and enlightening book which has made me reflect on how the universe can influence our lives.... the meditation exercises are very calming and I enjoyed listening to them.

Michelle (London)

"Inspiring, moving and immensely practical, Simon's book has the potential to change lives for the better."

Charlie Maclean
Author of Unforgettable

I've battled with depression for many years and have never turned to medication because I am genuinely against drugs. This book was the perfect tonic as everything recommended is easy to follow, natural and most importantly within your control. Simon, you have my gratitude, respect and admiration!

Ross (London)

The book is beautiful and you have bared your soul in order to help others and inspire them. I'm amazed at the way you've turned your own misfortune or sadness into a positive purpose to help others find their way. You certainly did that for me both in giving me this to read and with all the support you've given me over the last ten years that I've known you. I truly believe you are one of the few people that have been 'sent' to me ...special angels of protection here on this planet. Special friends who are totally 'tuned in' to higher influences and to human dilemmas...you have been a mentor, a therapist, healer, a rock, a guide and a true friend. Please accept my gratitude and thanks ....

Karren (London)

A very calm and enlightening read. Each paragraph offers so much that an individual can take a great deal, round by round.

The content offers a very positive outlook for the reader and has helped me look at my situation in a totally different way and am grateful for the positive input. This book would make a perfect gift for any loved one who needs positive help and I would be happy to recommend to all those of my friends who need such guidance.

Antony (Limassol, Cyprus)

Contents

Introduction..

This book came out of a spiritual vision to write a book and gave me the title, 'Out of the Dark', that took place 20 years ago and due to an event that happened in December 2014. I only started writing this book January 2015 and now in January 2016, it has become a reality and feel it is my true purpose in this life to share it with any poor souls in the dark!

They say that everyone has a story to tell and for me to have the desired effect on your life I need to tell you something about mine, so please bare with me..

To quote the author Mark Twain: **'The two most important days in your life are the day you were born and the day you find out why'.**

Just for the record, I went to one of the worst schools in the UK and by the time I left school, I could hardly do maths or read and write, as a result I don't read books and to date, have never read a newspaper in my entire life! So you might ask, how in God's name have I written this book?

Where to start? I guess the beginning would be a good place. Having a troubled childhood, with a father who would beat me up on a regular basis day after day and leading my entire youth in fear. He would beat my sisters too but not with the same intensity. He was a small man with a big mouth, big car, big boat, big shop, etc, yet above that big shop, my six sisters and I, along with my mum and dad, plus a big Alsatian dog would live in a ONE bedroom flat. My mum and dad would sleep on a divan bed in the front room and my six sisters and I would sleep in a small bedroom with two bunk beds, tripled up and filling the majority of the room and as the room was extremely tight, we would sleep top to tail, so you would wake up with the other family members feet in your face..

The big dog mauled me badly one day and my dad would not put the dog down and allowed it to go onto biting my sisters as well, needless to say, I have had a fear of dogs all my life, as a result.

I was told virtually every day by this father figure that I was a loser from a very tender age and that I would fail at everything I did. This has a very drastic effect on a young mind and as the mental and physical torture continued day by day and year by year, the pattern was becoming well impregnated in my entire body, mind and cells.. If this was not enough, I was sexually molested by our trusted babysitter on a regular basis. I wanted desperately to tell my mum but knowing she would obviously tell my father and feeling that he just would not believe me, that I would be in for yet another beating, so I had no alternative but to suffer in silence. Until writing this book, my mother and father, now passed away, never knew and my living sisters also never knew but they will do when they read this book.. That sort of stuff just got buried to the back of my mind with all the other shit!

Imagine being punished for no crime, going to prison guilty must be bad but going to prison innocent is hell and how I stayed out of that place in life only God knows.. The problem now is, you even doubt your own shadow and as much a brave face you put on and create a happy façade, the truth lay beneath and eventually something has to give. So the self doubt prophecy begins and the message that unknowingly goes out to the universe is one of self destruct!!

Clearly no one wants to admit defeat, so we fight for our own right to survive and attempt to uphold our integrity. So now survival kicks in by way of earning a living and wanting to prove to the tyrant of a father that he was wrong and I can make a success of my life and would do anything to prove I was worthy. I can tell you that I did virtually every job you could think of and just for the record here are the ones I remember, starting in order chronologically, doing the following jobs:

Paper round, delivering bread, working as a sales assistant in a toy shop, a sweet shop, in a market, life guard, women's hair salon washing hair and sweeping up, my uncle's trouser shop, John Colliers suit shop, Carnaby Street in fashion, for virtually every store in the street and became top salesman, Kings road in fashion, Oxford street in fashion, working for a T shirt company, cloakroom attendant, working behind a bar. Next I started in business for myself, in supplying printed T shirts to night clubs and bars, also to heat seal printed T shirts in Heathrow airport, only to have all my stock stolen within 24 hours and no insurance to cover the loss... I then became a fashion designer and supplying stores like Harrods, John Lewis etc, only to have the Italian factory that made my goods go behind my back and try to supply my outlets direct and cut me out, so I had to sever the relationship and seek other suppliers but could not. I moved on to teaching martial arts after becoming a black belt instructor, then to working as door security in top night clubs, after that getting into property and investing with some entrepreneur who conned me and my family and friends, so today I am having to deal with the stigma of the waves he created. Followed by selling Insurance for a leading Insurance company, only to find that the insurance company made some heavy losses and went down, at the same time putting me out of business. I had big income and big outgoings, only to end up with big outgoings and no income, I lasted 6 months and was made bankrupt and lost everything. Then to selling double glazing, selling gas and electric, doing telesales, after that creating a book of voucher offers for top companies like Avis, Holiday Inn, top restaurants, etc, which took a year to develop and it failed miserably, followed by designing a holiday club voucher membership but that failed too, then to becoming a personal trainer and teaching in a club, only for them to change the structure and decided to teach privately, then the gym where I taught closed down and had no facility to work from. I went back into property in 2007 and in 2008 the market crashed and lost everything again and became bankrupt for the second time. I returned to teaching health and fitness privately, which helped pay bills and more recently went into telesales for a friend, etc etc etc.. So you see, it's not for a lack of trying and I still stayed positive throughout but something kept blocking me and with my subliminal mind set in default, I appeared to be destined to failure. I tried so so hard along the way and found myself borrowing money or asking people to invest in my ideas, only to fail myself and them and needless to say, quick sand is awaiting!

Yet all through my teens, twenties, thirties, forties and fifties I managed to stay positive and keep up the fight and not give in, all this, until finally 4 years ago at the age of 59, I developed severe depression and the downward spiral began. I tried to fight it but it took hold in a massive way, it just got worse and worse, not being able to leave the house, not being able to look at people in the eye, going into panic on the motorways, panic and anxiety attacks, high blood pressure, you name it. Then my doctor prescribed anti depressants and I took just one tablet and had to call an ambulance for feeling dreadful and could not breathe. I did not take another tablet!

Then and only then did I really start to take a massive look at my life, what had I become or perhaps not become, how could I get this low. I have good entrepreneurial life skills, yet I was a sinking ship in every way you could possibly think... is this now my life over, is this the end of all my dreams and aspirations, is this darkness forever, now and in death. Only, and I mean only when I got to my absolute lowest point, did I get down on my knees and beg God for forgiveness for any and all mistakes I may have ever made, but asked him to look into my heart and see that I am a good person and only ever wanted to help mankind and to please help me, so that I may help other poor souls that are in the dark...

THIS was the moment when my life appeared to have meaning, some sudden jolt went through me, like an electric wave of inspiration and I think that due to my unselfish request, I felt I was actually heard and then answers started to appear, day by day... I was led every step of the way to fulfil my purpose, which is not to make money in any business but to relay my message and give hope to those poor souls in the dark, just as I was. I felt that spiritual guidance was pointing me in the right direction and brought certain people into my life at certain stages of this book, in order to deliver this book in the manner it would be best perceived and to have to have the best impact on its readers.

I have shared something very personal with you, in an attempt to reach out to you and let you know there are always hope and answers to the questions and in this book I will share with you, what got me into depression and what got me out of depression. I turned it all around and it would be my sincere pleasure to help you turn it all around too and get you out of the dark!

In this book I would like to share with you real experiences that took place and in my own way try to help you and let you know that I managed to turn it all around and all naturally.

Whilst depression is not sexist and women and men can have depression and there are many kinds and many levels, the bias in this book will appear to be more towards the male species purely as in the main, I am talking from my personal experiences but the desired solution is for both sexes.

There are brief chapters with situations and guidance to help you in your own lives, along with a tailored programme at the end of this book, that I have designed and which worked for me, in getting me out of depression, and I believe it will help you too, this will be your choice to follow the programme if you so desire.

Positive efforts bring positive results…. Negative efforts bring negative results!

This book is based on real time events and real experiences that have had monumental results and is not based on hypothetical hearsay.

The book has been presented in a manner to make it both easy to read and digest, using simple remedies, techniques and coping mechanisms… So it is my sincere hope that it has the positive effect in changing your life for the better. Your life, your future, your choice…

This book came out of a vision, that in time became reality and it is my heart-felt desire that it reaches all those poor souls in the dark, just as I was and… I believe in fate, especially if you are reading this book!

Out of the Dark: Round 1
A-bout depression

This book is not for anyone with a perfect life!

By contrast, it is hoped that this book helps those poor souls lost in the wilderness.

I too was in the dark and this story is about you and me!!

There are many types of depression, clinical, chemical, hormonal and many levels of depression, i.e., post-natal depression in women is just one type of the many forms, so male or female…depression is not sexist and we are all subject to its grip, even people who have a perfect life can suffer from depression…top actors, singers, footballers and even comedians like Robin Williams, so don't feel its exclusive to little old you! With this in mind, here is a famous quote by the late Robin Williams… **"I used to think the worst thing in life is to end up alone, it's not, the worst thing in life is to end up with people who make you feel alone".**

Through being at the depths of depression for many long years and wishing for death, yet some how in my DNA, I felt there was an answer out there, even though suicide was a temptation on more than one occasion, instinctively I knew there was this hope or certain faith I was supposed to hang onto... I must point out that I'm not religious, but perhaps spiritual now and feel there is a God or a universal life force and sometimes call upon this in my darkest hour, even though I can't see or touch it, I seem to know there is a presence. Anyway, more about the problem that we share or should I say shared?

After years of pain, heartache, depression, panic attacks, blood pressure, insomnia, anxiety, fear, not being able to go out, not being able to look people straight into their eyes, panic on the motorway when driving, feeling like giving up and not wanting to even get out of bed, the days seem long and the nights even longer... How much can we take and how long will it last.

Well my friend, I found the answer to this horrific problem and it would be my joy to share it with you, after all, how much do you want to get better, feel the sun on your face and welcome the beginning of each and every day?

So you are genuinely interested in getting out of this black hole then let's do this together...

I used to be the life and soul of the party and nothing bothered me, but with every knock in life there should be the upside of good things that happen, however, if there is a constant barrage of shit that over weighs you, then the balance of powers will shift and you will be on catch up with everyone else who seem to be doing well. I have had so much heartache in my life, I would not know where to begin, so I won't, just trust me, you have nothing to lose or rather you have? 'That dark heavy cloud over your head and in your heart.' We were not born with any of these feelings, they just manifest as more and more bad stuff happens, until we lose our way and identity, we forget why we were put on this vast and lonely planet after all. This is not going to be a light switch where you can turn the switch and all of a sudden you will be well but if you trust me and my logic, then you will be able to physically measure your own progress day by day, go from flat bottom to a percentage increase week by week. By the way, don't set yourself up for self sabotage by trying to see too much too soon, after all, you didn't get like this overnight and I can't do this for you, everyone has their own journey and much of this is free will and personal growth!

You may be wondering, so what's so special about his pain compared to mine, he doesn't know the pain I have been through and am still enduring. I only care about getting you feeling good again and that must be our main aim and mutual objective. Every day becomes the past and do you know what is special about today?? It's never been before! So we all stand a chance.

Losing my business, being made bankrupt twice, losing my home, furniture, cars, my wife leaving me for a wealthy guy when my business went down and left me alone to bring up our two young children on my own and with no help from anyone else, only to lose my daughter a few years later to an undesirable boy and now she's been gone 13 very long years. Losing friends, falling out with family, feeling cursed and what with having no money and trying to survive, I found myself having to make an onion, a tin of tomatoes and a bag of rice last a week!! Trust me, it's not easy, but I learned survival, yet getting so low and depressed, I was licking the fungi of the rubbish bin, in the hope I would become ill and die!

There were other thoughts of how I could do it, but something kept drawing me back and I was not entirely sure what was the message. Until I decided to ask for HELP! We cannot do this on our own, we are inverted and disappearing down a black hole, so we need to know when enough is enough and reach out. Oddly enough, there is always someone somewhere that will help, that is if you're genuine in wanting to be helped, otherwise, what's the point!

If you could feel good and actually say I feel good today, the chances are you would respond, 'Yeah but I know it's gonna be tuff', Well that's exactly what it will be, as the universe is a defined science and energy, therefore whatever you say or ask for, it might be something like "I bet today is going to be another crap day for me"… well the universe will conspire very hard to give you your wish, "oh great master!" Be careful what you wish for! … By contrast, the universe is not an idiot, if you say "today I'm gonna make a fortune" this wont happen on demand, well not straight away anyway and with your mind set in default mode, everything will be doomed, as your true inner belief will undermine your intention and cancel it out. Small changes with a shift in inner belief that start with the right intention will change your life graph exponentially! You will need to change your self -belief system to get you through the doubt barrier.

Back to me… there is such a thing as good and evil and evil can try to gain your soul, it tried on numerous occasions to get me to the dark side but I kept my faith in myself and the light, in God or some universal life force that I just can't explain, but I instinctively know it's out there. As time goes on I will reveal more.

After qualifying in many arts, Black belt Tae Kwondo instructor, Six years of studying Alexander Technique, Diplomas in Optimum Diet and Nutrition, Holistic healing, personal training, spiritual counselling, etc.…doing courses around the world and walking on hot coals! I was determined to excel... I ran many businesses that eventually all failed and invested and lost a great deal of money. I used to say, why me, why me, poor me poor me... Then eventually I stopped and looked at my life.

What was I missing???

What was I supposed to be thinking???

What was my purpose for being on this planet, in this universe at this time???

Then and only then did I get the answer...

Its quite simple (It's Purpose) Why are you here, why you, why now... because you have a purpose to be fulfilled...it could be to invent a medicine, climb a mountain, write a book to help others through depression or simply propagate the species to bring someone into the world who is special and has the golden child effect. Whatever the reason, there is always a reason and you need to look at your purpose and stop wallowing in a pool of self-pity!

When I was six years old, my very rich uncle said to me, "What do you want to do when you get older son?" Him thinking I was going to say an international banker or something on those lines, instead I said, 'I want to heal the world', his reply was, "that will be a neat trick!"

Not knowing quite what I meant at the time, I now know what my purpose is in life... not to make fortunes in business deals. The powers to be do not want me doing this and this was not my purpose or why I was put on the planet at this time. I realised that all my life skills and lessons I have learned have brought me to this point in time, to help you my good friend and I will!

Are you ready to want to help me to help you, to help the world help each other? … (I made up that saying myself, cool hey?!)

That is called the Butterfly effect and there will be irrevocable proof later in this book to show you without any shadow of doubt that all this is real, wonderful and doable, yes even you can achieve a sense of purpose and fulfilment.., yet I hear you say "Here we go again! Another offering of help, but I know how this will end in failure, despair and let down"…and you will be 100% right…especially if you say that! Because the universe has big ears and will hear exactly what you ordered from the catalogue!

Or you could lie through your teeth and say "Yes it works and I will be really positive and good things are with me now and in the future. You never know, you might even start to believe your own Bullshit! Ha Ha! …I was under pressure to go onto antidepressants, why not, half the nation is on them… but once again, something told me to avoid these man-made products and I believe there is always a cure and invariably it grows out of the ground. So I took purely natural remedies, practiced certain techniques and easy meditation and breathing exercises, along with other simple methods that I will teach you. I always wanted to be a teacher of life and sure you will have that ability too at some point.

So let's start by asking a simple question, "What is stronger, positivity or negativity? If I guessed right you would say positivity, right?

Well you would be wrong, the answer is **Negativity** and the reason why is you don't have to work at being negative... It's all around us, whereas you do have to work at being positive and that takes commitment... Remember, positive efforts bring positive results.

Negative efforts bring…?

We all have choices and can be in control of our own future, what's your choice??

Being in Prison

We can be in prison, either physically or mentally, either way we feel trapped and if you are physically in prison and struggling to stay in the game, then try to imagine that YOU are not actually in the prison but the prison is within you and you can control the situation with right thinking…If you have been at war for your country and are regretful of what you have done and find it hard to live with the feelings within you, then you need to re invent yourself and effectively re-program yourself to become someone new and say goodbye to the past.. We all do things we regret and we need to learn the coping mechanisms to get through.

Ill at ease

They say that when you are ill at ease, this creates disease and with enough negative situations occurring in your life, this will go into all the trillions of cells in your body and form a negative pattern. These cells are then programmed with your thoughts and where you program something to the negative, you can always re-program to the positive thoughts, so we are in control of our system.

Being in an abused situation is also a feeling of being in prison and there are different levels and types of abuse. Either way, you will feel persecuted and hit on and the effects can run extremely deep. So learn how to switch off from this torment and be in control of your emotions. The techniques shown further into the book will help with all this.

When we think of being down, there is a small part of us that feels we could get better but there is a large part of us that will argue that right out the door...it's as if we are content being in this cocoon of sorrow and comfortable in our solitude. So something has to change and to make change oddly enough it means you have to have greater pain, because we only act when the pain is too great and cannot tolerate things anymore, so I'm hoping your pain is heavy enough so we can get some bloody work done and get you smiling again.

There are many ways back to normality and I would suggest that you will need many of those ways and therapies to get back. One therapy alone is most unlikely to set you right and don't think for one minute that you will have an easy ride, this is going to take EFFORT from you and others will help you on your journey so you won't be alone...Oh and by the way ... I am here all the way home

Out of the Dark: Round 2
Digging Deep

So are we ready to go round 2 and get in the mix? With all this depression malarkey you have to box clever, otherwise you will end up taking a battering that can be avoided.

As mentioned, it's all about learning specific techniques that will help you get through your day and if you are anything like I was, then the thought of getting through one day in itself was pressure enough, so we will plan our day backwards. The reason for this is because we need to be realistic as to the outcome of all that stress, despair and lack of simple confidence that leaves us when we need it most, normally in front of someone or even in a crowd. This will slowly wear you down as the day goes on and by the end of the day you will be on your reserve batteries. How can we overcome these feelings, again techniques are the answer, along with natural remedies and coping mechanisms.

You know, through life's hardship and brutal lessons, we either learn or crumble and I made up a saying along the way and even today it holds me in good stead.. I remember being Mr. Positive and when things turned so bad, became Mr. Negative… the latter is easier to achieve than the former but there has to be a more realistic approach to how we assimilate our feelings, therefore here is the saying I made up.

'I used to be optimistic, then I became pessimistic, now I've became realistic' and it's that sense of realism that will keep you on a more even keel throughout your day and offer you the chance to build on days and weeks, after all, anything worthwhile is worth waiting for but don't be too patient, we have work to be done getting you to promote my book to everyone you know and help make me rich :) not just with money but with the joy of changing a life for the positive and hopefully you will smile when you think of how we turned this all around together.. I won't give up on you, so you don't give up on me either, deal? x

Let's access your feelings right at this moment, 'is this guy for real or is this false hope', after all, your comfort zone is staying low in your cocoon of pity, or 'is this guy for real and should I dedicate my efforts to actually wanting to feel good, after all what have I got to lose., well I could sink lower and that is something I really don't want or just maybe he has hit the nail on the head and with his help to walk me through the quagmire of shit, I am prepared to make an effort.'… I will do my 100% best to make you better, at least meet me half way so we both stand a chance!!

So this is where I would say that is not good enough, why you might ask? The answer is simple, if you say you will try and then you fail, then you can say, 'at least I tried', I don't want you to try at all. I want you to do! Then you won't fail. Simples hey!

Now we focus on the end of the day backwards, because we will need to prepare our feelings or at least be prepared for how we would normally have felt by the end of the day and at that point you would normally want to call it a day!

These will all be small steps that will give you the ability to change the thoughts from negative to positive and find a doable balance to make life worth living again.

I remember one summer day looking up at a clear blue sky, the sun shinning on my face, yet it was raining in my heart, how could I get this low? Now the sun charges me with energy, warmth, needed vitamins and I get a sun tan to boot and when I look in the mirror with a bit of colour in my face, I look that bit better, so instinctively feel better and so on. So these are small changes that will all mean more as we progress.

It's all about changing your frame of mind and working with the universe and a higher force if you believe in this presence. As mentioned, I am not religious, but cannot help but call upon this presence in my darkest hour and although this force must have a lot on its plate I believe that God eventually gets around to me.

I have done many courses around the world, as I have a thirst for a certain type of knowledge and can tell you that I have NEVER read a newspaper in my life, as I am not interested in that type of knowledge and that won't feed my soul but I am interested in the planet, the universe and anything that helps me to help you, as that is my purpose on this beautiful planet of ours

One of the seminars I went on was the great Anthony Robbins, who is a wonderful motivational speaker and one of the things he said was that "we don't learn out of pleasure, only pain", which seems quite sad but true...for example, if you and I were going to have a race to the end of the street, who would win? Well obviously I would, because I'm more positive, right?... But how about if ask my Japanese martial arts expert with a long sharp Samurai sword to run behind you, with instructions for him to cut you into shreds if you don't win! Now do you think you might run faster and even beat me?? You see we will do little to gain pleasure but virtually anything to avoid pain, so let pain be the leverage to get you to win!! Only one of two things will give you success, either inspiration or desperation, anything in between won't motivate you sufficiently.

Out of the Dark: Round 3
Keeping Your Defences Up!

So far I have touched on a few things that may resonate with you and once again, don't think because nothing else has worked in the past, that what we are doing here will have the same effect.

Please remember this saying... "The past does not equal the future". In other words, no one can control the past but '**you** can control **your** future!

I tend to make references that you can go back to quite frequently in this book and that will help you keep your finger on the pulse and don't end up with any anti-climax or finale. We shall remain always active and always improving! There will be phrases and positive affirmations that will give you meaning and inspiration, along with specific direction.

So here is another while we are on the subject… By the way, this is for you to say and put your heart and soul into this one.

"I am getting better and better, every day in every way'…and you might want to thank the universe for its help.

These are all positive affirmations and the more time you spend in the positive now, the less time you will have to loiter in the negative past!

Now let's get you on the road to recovery and happiness.. I mentioned in an earlier section that techniques and natural remedies play a vital role in changing you from depressed to creating your personal coping mechanism. Firstly let me state for the record, I am not a medical doctor who would recommend anti depressants and I'm not here to say that the medical profession would not act in your best interest but you can read all the side effects that these man made products produce… like feelings of depression, feelings of suicide, insomnia, panic attacks etc. In addition, they may make your immune system redundant and you may become dependent on these, so after a while you may have to up the dosage.

The bottom line is, I don't claim to be a medical expert, nor do I doubt those that recommend these drugs have ever experienced depression, whereas, you and I most certainly have (we are the experts in depression), and only we can know how deep the rabbit hole goes?

One of the methods that you may wish to adopt is creative visualisation whilst breathing, this is both easy and free. Take time in the day, preferably once in the morning when you awake and last thing at night before you fall asleep.

I made this up myself and know it works for me and should work for you too…

Sit in a quite place and close your eyes, allow your body to give into your planet's gravity and let yourself feel heavy, take a slow breath in for 5 seconds and slowly out for 6 seconds. Imagine yourself inside a gentle waterfall of smooth cool water and as the sun shines through the waterfall, it creates a rainbow and then you will be bathing in all the colours of what nature provides for free and with love.. This you can do for about 5 minutes and remember to come back ... If you struggle a little with this, then I have developed an easy meditation CD, where I talk you through the meditation, it is backed with some soft therapeutic music that will help you relax.

Lastly, to change your state of mind, you need to change how you think, where you go usually and what you do in any given day.. What you do is pattern forming and any link to where you go and what you do, can remind you of how you felt at that time and in that place. So we need to build new patterns and break the links to the past patterns.

Affirmations.

Affirmations are very powerful and strong intent will help make them real. Get yourself a large pad, around A4 size and every night prior to going to bed take two pieces of paper, on one piece write down all the bad things that happened in the entire day on the other piece of paper wright down all the good things that happened in the same day. Against all the good things write a large tick and a smiley face and on the paper with the bad things put a cross and a sad face.

Then take the paper with the bad stuff and tear it into little shreds and throw in the bin with contempt and put two fingers up and say good riddance and see this as a positive stand that you don't care anymore...

This will create a massive statement in your mind and send out a positive statement to the universe that you are taking back your control over your life and destiny!

Needless to say, there are many ways to find healing for ourselves, we just have to search within ourselves to WANT TO FIND THE ANSWERS...with that in mind, you can attend a medium or clairvoyant and maybe try to get some guidance that way and perhaps attend a spiritual gathering, where like minded people are looking for answers about who they are and where they should be going. I have attended many and have had great help in many ways, for those that feel something that may of effected themselves, that could be of a bad spirit, there are those that can help lift these negative energies.

Prayer

Whatever your beliefs and or religion, there are many of us that believe that prayer may be the strongest way to get help and whoever your God maybe, there is no harm in asking for that help, however please bear in mind, that sincerity in what you ask for should be real and heartfelt, otherwise what's the point and who would listen to a half baked prayer.

Please remember, it's not all about you and you taking, it's also about giving!

For most of my life I believed there was a God but had my doubts and bearing in mind, I am not here to tell you to believe in God, only to relay my thoughts, after all, when we are faced with a massive crises, do we not tend to say, Oh my God or God help me? That is a knee-jerk reaction, yet somehow we instinctively feel something and the more pain we are in mentally, the more we tend to want to ask for help. I started to be more sincere and less selfish about how I asked and eventually I was heard and my life changed for the better, bearing in mind I have mentioned previously in this book that I am not religious and remain the same.

Prayer will bring you closer to your maker and will help give you purpose and just maybe you may find out who you have come here to be and what your true purpose is on this earth.

That's your lot for today. Do your best and make me proud of you

Out of the Dark: Round 4
A Star in The Making

Right at this moment you might be pondering certain questions in your mind, that's how doubt and negativity works. Questions may formulate from the doubt and negative thought process. Questions can either be positive or negative. I feel if you ask the right question, the Universe will give you the right answers, however, ask questions that are negative and you will get a negative response. If no questions are raised there will not be answers. Think of the Universe as a receiver to what we emit.

So, lets think about questions that are both relevant and constructive. We hit on this in a previous round, but let us ask the main questions, you should be saying, Why me? Why now? Why was I born me? The answer lays within each individual, as we are all on an individual journey and it should be about personal growth, fulfilment and purpose, but you might say, "I'm just an ordinary person in an ordinary town". Ok, let's examine how unimportant you may think you are.

Let me take you on a journey back in time, roughly 14.5 billion years ago when the universe set off the big bang and you were not quite formed yet. :)

Through billions of years the Universe has been constantly growing and changing and forming new stars and planets.. Through modern technology, man can now plot most of the known universe through mathematics and whilst the majority of the vast universe is matter and empty space, we understand this space to be dark matter and or dark energy and the rest is visible matter that we are still learning about.

There are roughly 200 billion stars in our galaxy, the Milky way, and there are trillions of galaxies in an infinite Universe with as many or if not more stars. With our very own sun at the centre of our solar system. When it ignited roughly 4.5 billion years ago, exploding out debris and gaseous clouds, these eventually coalesce via gravity to form planetoids and ultimately, our own mother earth. Then from the heavy bombardment period, we were a ball of hot larva, eventually cooling, only to have another giant structure collide with us that caused a massive shock that put us into another melt down period and that large giant structure that hit us was our own moon, that today plays a major part in our every day lives and without it, we would cease to exist. So you see, when the sun ignited and sent all of that mass out, we came into formation, so effectively, we were born out of our very own sun and surely are made up of many of the trace minerals that exist on the sun, on the earth and in our own bodies. Our planet oscillates at roughly 1600kph and hurtles through space to circumvent our sun at around 66,000 mph. It takes us 365 days to complete this massive journey and we arrive back at the same place without fail every year. Wow wow wow! Yet do you feel you are moving?? What an amazing miracle! Do you not feel that you might just be a bit special to even witness this miracle, let alone be on the planet to go along for the ride of a life time!!!

Then there is the Goldie Locks effect, where we have just the right amount of gravity, roughly 1g… less than this and we would be flying off into the unknown and more than 1g and we would be crushed, so it's just perfect to keep our feet firmly planted on the ground. We also are in a part of the galaxy and solar system where we are close enough to the sun to have the right amount of heat so we don't burn to a crisp, and just the right distance away so we don't freeze into pure ice. Without the perfect distance, no plants would grow and life itself would not exist… Our atmosphere has an abundance of oxygen… without it nothing would live and thrive. Mother earth has its magnetic fields protecting us from solar radiation, along with our rich atmosphere which also protects us from unwanted flying giant meteors and asteroids etc., and yet years prior, it is believed that some of these meteors and asteroids brought liquid water to our planet and ultimately helped create living organisms, US! These are just some of the building blocks for Life!

Another interesting fact, is that in order for our sun to heat our distant planet, over 93 million miles away, it converts and burns hydrogen into helium at a rate of 600 million tons a second! And all of this dynamic energy is so we can stay warm and get a suntan…the miracle goes on!

Planet Earth is a vast miracle where man has been struggling to find any planet in the entire galaxy that has these Goldie Locks perfect living conditions and none exist.

So, why you? Why now? Why here? Perhaps you just got lucky...or perhaps the creator found a place in his heart for you

To have meaning and peace of mind, you need to think outside the box and wonder why you and why now, then count your lucky STARS that you are one of the chosen ones. Stop doubting your special meaning for being brought into existence now and question only what your purpose for being here may be ...start believing in who you are. Depression is deep thought... spend your deepest thoughts on the bigger picture.

Find joy in your every day, enjoy your planet and now you have your life and purpose, perhaps you can start to realise that there is something quite wonderful going on and you simply have to be part of this extraordinary journey and celebrate life, your life!

We will continue to assist you in finding your purpose, just be patient and keep your positive belief system, the rest will become clearer as we progress with this together..

Out of the Dark: Round 5
Throwing in the towel

If you're in the state that I was in only a year ago, you would probably be thinking, I just am so fed up and so low, I can't see myself giving this the attention it requires to get myself back on track and think its probably not even gonna work anyway, so might as well save myself the upset now, than go through all this pain to be let down at the end. You see that is the logic and mind set of a pessimist and you have earned that title. So the answer from me is simple.. Read it, Don't read it.. it's your choice! Knowing your state of mind as I knew mine, I would not blame you!

On the flip side of that coin, you will also be thinking deep down into the last fraction of any positivity that you may have left in you, what if this is the one to get me to feel good again and what if I'm giving up that chance to turn me around. So I will spell it out for you in simple language.

Repeat these very technical words after me…. Whatever! What have I got to lose, apart this crap feeling!
Anyway, moving on now after a temporary relapse, we have work to do champ!

You may notice that I refer to the chapters as rounds and by now you must know that you in a fight for your life and I am your corner man, encouraging you on and inspiring you with every blow in life you take, and the loud voice in your ear is me telling you to keep your spirits up and box clever.

Throwing in the towel…I was sitting in the sauna and was looking for inspiration for something to express my thoughts about round 5, as to what you may be feeling at this moment in time and where I sat on the bench in the sauna, I placed my towel next to me on my left, only to notice that someone had been sitting there and had left a pool of water where they had sweated probably last nights drinking session and decided to throw my towel with disgust to a lower level… at that moment it gave me the inspiration of the title for round 5, Throwing in the towel! You see there are signs everywhere and guidance is always around us but sometimes we are blind to the signs or not in the right frame of mind to recognise them, so be aware that help is always at hand.

Throwing in the towel…you would have heard this expression and it has multiple meanings but they all come back to the same thing… giving up!

I was so many times ready to call it a day, but being somewhat intuitive and spiritual, felt sure that the lessons are for us to learn and we have to fight through them and gain our personal growth and if we decide to bail out early, then the main question will be asked by the powers to be above, did this person learn the lesson we sent them to earth to learn, (NO) in which case you will probably be reincarnated back into the same person or situation and have to go through all that pain all over again, until you (DO) learn that lesson. So for God's sake, 'Man up' and make the fight worthwhile and win!

Contrary to your belief, you are a very special person and especially to me. I know your plight and the darkest journey that you are facing, but if you can trust me that I have been through all that you may be going through and maybe a lot worse than you, yet through strength, determination, faith in our friend upstairs and faith that I knew I was special, special enough to reach out to you and make a special difference in your life, then let this be a sign that you are not alone and I am with you on your difficult journey and we will together win the fight.

Remember the last thing in Pandora's box was hope, so keep your faith in who you are and who you have come here to be. When you are yourself again, and you will be, then you can return the favour one day to me, by taking your success and helping another poor soul to change their life for the better... and you would have now achieved your purpose in your life and love will fill your heart and make you proud of who you have become.

Out of the Dark: Round 6
Half Empty or Half Full?

We are now half way and you are in one of two minds now and both are stated above, so we have free will and choices and I cannot have your thoughts for you, that is what makes you special to you and in many ways unique!

So this is where your mind and emotions come into play and perhaps the most difficult part to master.

If you set realistic goals you are less likely to have your boat rocked, so take small steps and know your own limitations. The idea is not to make you 100% better but to get you to a level where you can operate comfortably. I have mastered the art of nothingness, in that I don't look for anything, I just allow it to be and leave the deeper emotions to one side. For example, there will be songs that will remind you of good and sad situations, yet we have to be a bit more realistic than that, after all, any song that you heard before today is past memories and virtually all will remind you of how it was before or what you had before, good and bad, so changing your state of mind and new songs must anchor better feelings for you. Then there are films, this will be the same issue, then there are places, same issue, then there are people you know, same issue and so on. The key is to limit yourself to the negative exposure and lean towards things that keep you safe from mental torment.. For example, stay away from people that effect your energy in a negative way.. When a dog knows you are afraid, it is more likely to bite you!

So now we need to prepare ourselves in advance of the activity... Lets say you're watching a love film and you remember when you were in love and someone broke your heart... 'Stop!' This is a 'no-no' and you can't put yourself through this type of mental torment, horror movies certainly will not put you in a stable frame of mind and are most unlikely to feed your soul.. So in this category you should only watch comedy!

A study by the university of California, took a large number of manic depressives and moved them out of their current environment and took them to a beautiful building of bright happy colours... the building allowed lots of natural light to come in through large windows and the grounds were lush green with beautiful trees, bushes, flowers and fountains with running water. They had happy staff, they had comedians come in to entertain them, played comedy films, gave them holistic therapies like massage reflexology etc., and made them feel good about themselves. When the experiment or study was complete, virtually everyone was cured of their depression, apart from a few stubborn fools that would not allow them-selves to want to get better.

Another are warning signs...there will or maybe times when a certain environment becomes uncomfortable and you feel you're losing the edge or that certain control you had previously…when this happens, you need to have a back up plan and that for me would be to say your just popping to the loo, when in fact you go outside, get some oxygen and focus on the trees, the sky and easy breathing and reset your thermostat, so you can get back into the game.. This is in no way admitting defeat… it's being realistic about getting back on track again.

For one moment, imagine your brain is a computer and you have been given a computer virus. After all, it is us as humans, with human brains that created and program computers, they did not invent us!!!

In this case, we need to become a little more robotic and try to leave emotion out of the equation and reboot our own mind computer, and once we have eliminated the so called virus, then we re-program ourselves to see things differently, with less pain and emotions. Once you have mastered this, you can bring back emotions gradually.

In the Japanese culture you may never see a picture of a sunset, as this represents the end, it's over…. by contrast they prefer to have pictures of a sunrise, a new beginning, a new start, it's even on their countries' flag for proof. So learn from these simple illustrations and start to build your own jigsaw puzzle and make the pieces how you want them to fit!

I have learned many of these techniques and am probably 80% better and that is more than enough to have happiness. This is not to impress you but to impress upon you, that everyone has control over their own destiny, mind and emotions if they truly wish to and you will do it too!

Further Affirmations

As mentioned, affirmations are a good and positive way to re-program the thoughts of the mind which are the main computer...Affirmations such as – I ask the Universe to take away any doubt, fear or negativity within me and around me and ask the Universe to take it away from me and place it somewhere safe, so it can be disposed of organically...in return please send me strength, courage and positivity in and around me, with protection from any negative energies (and then give thanks).

Another good one is – I am so grateful I was born me, I am gifted, I am good, I am special, and no-one else on this entire planet was born me...I deserve happiness and love.

Yet another confirming affirmation to yourself is to look directly into a mirror, deep into your own eyes, point your index finger directly at the reflection of yourself, and repeat the following:

"I am going to get better and better every day in every way... and this is my pledge."

Well done for getting past half way, now you're half full.

Out of the Dark: Round 7
The Sucker Punch

In boxing terms there is an expression called the sucker punch and it's where we get caught with our guard down, in other words we leave ourselves exposed to unnecessary risk that will cause us ultimate pain. These can be the following: Drugs, Booze, Gambling etc., and whilst these are addictions, they are also lessons in life.

Booze... there is social drinking and there is addiction, where you have to drink to stay in the game... If you are taking any natural remedies, then these will help, however any mainstream medication does not mix well with alcohol and will have an adverse effect, in addition, the booze will affect your overall health in the short and long term. I'm not here to tell you to give it up, that is down to free will but you may wish to consider just drinking on the weekends for a while and once a month doing a 1 week detox. Milk thistle will help detox your liver, if its not too late :(

Hardcore drugs… not having ever tried any drug, I would not know the addictive side of things but if you are caught in their web, then you may wish to ask yourself, where you are going and where you anticipate ending up on your present path…

Gambling… we all want to get rich quick and sometimes what looks like innocent fun tends to take us over and the bookies always win, so no doubt we will lose, then you end up chasing yesterday's losses. I too got caught in that downward spiral and lost a heap of money until the pain got too great and only then did I get the message, so hopefully you have accumulated enough losses and pain to walk away, there is no shame in walking away, only shame if you stay!

With any and all addictions, comes stress, anxiety, panic and guess what, depression…If you are in anyway lost in the wilderness and want out, then there are people out there always willing to help, so don't be too proud to ask.

Replacement

If you wish to change your life for the better and empty out these addictions, then there will be space that needs to be replaced. This is a time of positive change and you will probably need and want something worthwhile to do, so that you know you are going forward… HEALTH is a good one, so get a diary and plan to hit the gym for a workout at least 3/4 times a week… if you can use a combination of light weights and cardiovascular exercise, at least 20 minutes… this will induce endorphins which will help you feel good… swimming is good for you and relaxing, there are also classes like Pilates and Yoga which will help you physically and spiritually, then there are sauna's, steam rooms and whirlpools to help you relax… with all that extra money you will have for not paying for your addictions. You will now start to see some benefit from your money, helping to get you on track to getting you well again.

Spend 30 minutes a day doing relaxing meditation to calm and centre yourself. Then there are hobbies… Golf, Tennis, Football, Badminton, Squash, Netball, the list is endless and you may have fun too!

If you're not working then perhaps a part time job to bring in some extra money and whilst you're working your mind will be occupied.

Gaps in your day will effect gaps in your confidence, so plan your day backwards so there are no unexpected lows that will leave you lacking.

Its important to focus on what you DO want in your life, in addition, its important to be aware of what you DON'T want in your life!

Your life is going to get better and you will be the one to take all the praise…

Out of the Dark: Round 8
You V Negativity

We are now at round 8 and the best part of the way home and you should be getting a feel for this now.

The path we tread is a lonely one. The days are long and the nights even longer, especially with numb thoughts that rotate around our minds, regurgitating the same thoughts over and over again and searching, searching for answers, but to what?

As stated in previous chapters, I am not religious and do not attend any services, however I do believe in a higher force and for me that is God, and whoever your God maybe, if your prayers are heartfelt and sincere, then I truly believe you will connect and get the divine intervention you need, even if the help that comes may not be quite what you had in mind at the time, however this should always be for the highest good.

I was going to write about something I thought of previously today but was guided to offer something entirely different, so bear with me...

Approximately 20 years ago I lost my world... my business went down, I lost my home, my furniture, cars, bankruptcy and my wife left me and my children for some rich guy ...all in one go. I was so low that I considered taking my life on more than one occasion. I was numb!

Even in that numbness, I was guided to a counsellor. She was very kind to me, yet every time I arrived at her doorstep, when she opened the door I didn't remember how I got there, yet I made it every week without fail.

She cried every time I saw her, she said she could feel my pain and it was too much for her to contain. Somehow she knew the type of person I was even then and that somehow there was a calling within all this despair and told me every week, I know the pain you are going through and I promise you, a sign will come, a sign will come. I did not understand nor did I care to be honest. I only knew that I was lost in the wilderness, lost and alone. Every week that I would see her, there were certain things that would stay in my mind and one in particular was that someone cared, I mean genuinely cared and wanted to help me. I don't know how I found her but someone or something was guiding me. Each time I arrived, we turned right into this small room that only had one small window that was to my right where I would normally sit. A big part of me did not want to be there, not wanting to own up that my marriage had failed and that I had lost everything, moreover, I did not want to admit that I was a failure.

I had now been seeing this counsellor for about 6 or 7 weeks and still in pain. The room was always slightly dark and with only one small window not much light could come in. I remember arriving one late November day... it was really cold, damp, dark and miserable, just what I needed to help my feelings! I went inside and the room was even darker than usual. I looked out the window and the sky was black with clouds miles thick and made things even more depressing. I looked across from me and the lady counsellor was weeping and she gave me a saying to remember and I remember it to this very day. 'Few things matter much, and most things don't matter much at all' With that, whilst weeping, she said again, I know your pain darling and I promise you a sign will come. Now I was getting quite upset with her, as she kept saying this worthless comment and it had no meaning to me whatsoever! Then something very strange happened, at that exact moment when she made the comment, a light came through the window, which did not register with me, especially as there was no sun visible through miles of thick rain clouds. The light was extremely white, not like sunlight at all and it was near blinding... It made the room totally light up and the only way I could explain it was 'heavenly'.... It only lasted a few seconds and then the light went completely. At that exact moment when the light happened, I got the weirdest message somehow, it was that I should write a book, it did not say what about or give me any ideas, but from somewhere in my tiny brain it gave me this title 'Out of the dark'. That was 20 years ago and apart from writing a few notes that didn't amount to anything apart from to remind me, I had no inclination to write anything at all. For all the years now gone past, I thought about the book but nothing came through and was getting a bit frustrated with something that was so monumental to start and ended up as an anti climax. 17 years later I got heavy depression and battled with this for 3 years... I took just one anti-depressant tablet and had to call an ambulance as I felt so terrible...after then

I would not take anti depressants and decided to conquer this with natural remedies and holistic therapies... Because things were so bad I even would kneel at the side of my bed every morning and night and pray to God for help, then my prayers went from personal help, to please God let this be a lesson to me so that I may help others.. Then I started to get better and become more in control of my mind and emotions, to the point I felt that I could now start to write the book that would help others in their depression.

But I still couldn't...

As mentioned previously, that I went to a really bad school and when I left, could hardly read, write or do maths, so the idea of writing a book was not something I welcomed.

The story does not end there and by the last chapter you will understand what magical event happened to change all that. Be patient and don't go to the end of this book, as you still have work to do before this part is revealed.

Out of the Dark: Round 9
A good corner man

We are now three quarters of the way through and that much nearer to you being that much better percentage-wise. Remember we are not looking for a 100% improvement... that would be unrealistic and would only lead to a let down, instead we are looking for a small percentage of changes every day, that on your life graph will give you a more realistic and sustainable frame of mind.

Thoughts are things

Thought is everywhere and the thoughts you think attract the same in reality, however most people don't see this as they can't comprehend that what they are thinking is becoming their environment and their way of reality. Like attracts like and these are in essence the laws of attraction... the thoughts you think become things in your every day life. Therefore, if you send out a thought to the universe like... 'Why do things always go wrong in my life?' The universe will conspire to give you a definitive response... 'Because your a loser'.... but that's not what you really meant, so you will have to rephrase the question from 'why do things always go wrong in my life?', to 'how can I make my life more worthwhile?'... now the universe must respond to a more constructive question and deliver the answer in a way that will give you the inspiration to go forward, instead of backward, so the reply will be something like 'Stay in a positive state of mind no matter what, and plan your life as you would want it to be'. So we need to creatively visualise what we really want in our lives, rather than waiting for the phone to ring or a letter to arrive to hopefully change it for us. We need to take full control of what we truly desire for ourselves and via creative visualisation we can master our thoughts and control where, what and how. It's your life and no one can live it for you, so make yours a worthwhile life.

A good corner man

When we refer to a good corner man, it is understood that someone is fighting our cause and just like when I sought help from the lady counsellor that I went to see, you can do the same. Talking is therapy and having someone to listen who is not judgmental and is there to help is always a good start. Friends are a good point of contact, yet there is only so much that a friend can handle and as we all have our own problems, we have to be sympathetic to the fact that friends will only be able to cope with so much and ultimately you will need the expertise of a qualified counsellor to listen and give the right responses for your individual circumstances. If money is a problem, then your GP may be able to refer you, and these days CBT (Cognitive Behaviour Therapy) is the modern day form of therapy... they may be able to assist you in your mission to get back on track. Remember talking is therapy and it's important to get off your chest what is on your mind... during this process you will say 'words' and words are things.... this is what you have created in your mind and in your world.. (just as you have created this form of reality you live in), **you have the ability change your thoughts to a more congruent reality for how you want life to be for YOU!**

Re-programming

Just like a computer can be reprogrammed, our brains can be reprogrammed too... After all, our brains are highly sophisticated computers, far more effective than the best computer on the market...

Why? Because we program computers!!

We are the inventors... we gave life... we give our imprint and the basic knowledge and the computer then speeds up the solution, this is normally by maths and not by reasoning, as the computer does not have a heart nor does it know emotion... it is clinical and effective. Therefore take a leaf out of its book and re-program your own circuits to give you maximum results!!

In control, remember that we function out of emotion, so leave the letter E out of Emotion and just deal with life as Motion... that way you will have more control over your sensitivity to awkward events and situations.

The pieces of the jigsaw are starting to all fall into place and you will be getting a clearer picture of who you need to become to be the new you. Keep up the good work... we are nearly there!

Out of the Dark: Round 10
If You Wanna Win You Have to Planet

As I write the chapter this morning, we are celebrating a partial eclipse of our sun, which is eclipsed by our moon and today is March the 20th, so its also the first day of Spring, it's also a super moon, as the moon is the closest to us in many years and its gravitational pull on our planet is at its greatest. Bearing in mind, this is a miniscule fraction of what is going on in our Galaxy, let alone the entire universe..!

Today we will explore the difference between our planet and the people that sit on it and you my friend are one of those lucky few.

Firstly let's deal with depression and "does the planet have depression?"… well I would say it does.

Man cannot be satisfied with what he or she has and there are those that will take more than their fare share and steal the planet of its natural resources, in the process will

45

disturb the natural equilibrium of its dynamic flow. Imagine sucking the life blood out of mother earth and then asking her to be beautiful and blossom, it's almost a contradiction in terms. This may not appear to be overly relevant to you right at this very moment but it will become so shortly, so bear with me for now.

Everything is connected... that means this earth, the gravitational pull of the planet Jupiter, and the Meteor that is due to come within thousands of miles within her gravity. You may ask, what's this got to do with me? Well it's quite simple... that meteor had your name on it and it's the end of your life as you know it, however, one of the wonders of the universe was at work... and that is... gravity and Jupiter pulled that meteor of its course, and instead of landing on your fragile head Jupiter used its colossal gravity to pull the meteor off its present course and take the hit directly.

There is a message in this process and you may wish to look at the bigger picture now... and here is a saying you may wish to consider. 'The fact the rock fell was an accident. The fact the rock fell while you were under it was no accident!'

So all this was avoided by some galactic phenomenon... you were saved and clearly it was not your time to perish. Consequently, you should be extremely grateful that it was not your time to be eliminated and you are very much still in the game.

Does the planet give us depression?

Today is a partial solar eclipse and proves that the universe is always moving and as we are on a planet in space, we also are moving with it... but ask yourself a question... if I am on a beautiful planet that rotates at thousands of kilometres an hour, does this give you depression? The fact that the earth travels around the sun at over 66,000 mph and 365 days later ends up back at the same spot every year, does this give you depression? The answer clearly is NO...Without this most wonderful event, the earth would either burn to a cinder or we would freeze to death.

It gives us our seasons and nature does the rest... Just think of the four seasons… the winter gives us snow and ice… ice will kill off bacteria and help propagate new seeds… also you can go skiing.

The summer will give you lighter and brighter and warmer days and you can go on holiday and get a tan. Autumn will give us an abundance of varied colours in the leaves and this is when the leaves will fall, only to bring us into Spring, when new buds will spring into life and flower for us to marvel at, this in turn will put a spring in our step and represent new life and a new beginning… We only have to go along for the ride and unlike a fairground ride this one is free and far more rewarding!

So let's further this theory… if the wind blows, does this give depression? If the rain makes the flowers grow with the help of the sun, does this give you depression? If lightning strikes does it give you depression? Well clearly the answer is NO, because these are all natural events and we are a part of nature and its wonders, in fact any event that happens with our planet is not designed to give us depression and we are a part of the wonders of the universe. So if that's the case, then what does give us depression?

Well the only thing left are the <u>people</u> on the planet and the <u>situations</u> that they cause, and the cause and effect… in other words we respond in either positive or negative to positive or negative people, and their actions towards us and situations we find ourselves in, as a result of these interactions, it can slowly wear us down and cause depression. If this is the case, then we must choose who we interact with and see the warning signs in advance of the interaction.

We are only human. With this in mind, we must know that we have limitations as to what we are able to suffer, and constant pressure will slowly drag us down, after all, how much can one take... and with enough of the wrong things happening we will find ourselves overwhelmed and slowly slip down the slippery path.

So how can we turn all this around you may ask... Remembering, I too was suffering from severe depression and managed to turn this all around without the need of man made anti depressants... So surely nature is the answer!!! Do everything you can to get back to mother nature and move away from the rate race that put you in this state in the first place.

So what are some simple steps we can take? Here is just one of the first... Putting your face in the sun for just 10 minutes a day will help to recharge your batteries. My theory is the Sun, our Sun, burns at millions of degrees centigrade burning all of its Hydrogen and Helium, and with millions of tons of gravity, causes enough chemical reactions to form all the basic elements like Cobalt, Carbon, Copper, Zinc, etc., some of the building blocks of life, all the way down to some of the more valuable elements such as Gold, Silver, Uranium etc..... and these elements are in all of us!

So when you get the rays from our Sun on your body from over 90 million miles away, it helps restore and re-charge these chemical elements that we are made up of, and will make you feel more positively charged. Remember if you shine the brightest torch from 9 miles away you will hardly see a spec, yet something 90 million miles away can light up a world and give you life! By the way, the comments in this section above about the Sun's elements are my own conclusions and I have not taken reference for this from anywhere.

The next is a blue sky, just seeing it will help a reaction in your retina and the natural light blue will help increase happy hormones in you.

Running water is another therapeutic remedy to make you feel more relaxed and more positive. Roughly 70% of the planet is water, roughly 70% of what we eat and drink is water, and 70% of our bodies are water, so surely we feel at home when we are around water, whether it's the sea, a lake, a stream or a water fall, we are more relaxed when near water and nearer to nature again.

Trees are one of natures wonders, giving us oxygen and bearing fruit for us to eat or leaves to admire or shade under. Spend more time nearer to trees and if possible, hug an oak tree for strength but do ask for permission from the tree first, as it is a living organism just like you and has its own feelings.

Feng Shui…having the right energy in the place you live and work in can affect your energy.. Too much clutter and the positioning of certain factors can play a vital role in the positive and negative energy flow where you live and sleep.

There is much information free online regarding Feng Shui and it's worthwhile seeing how you could improve factors in your living space. The wrong energy where you stay can affect your energy, for bad or good, so it's worthwhile looking into the ancient belief system and philosophy.

Flowers are an abundance of life and colour and so varied, seeing various colours is pleasing to the eye and if you are out of work, apply for a job in a garden centre or as a park keeper, where you get to work with nature and get paid too.

Go for walks in the fresh air... the air is free and you will get some exercise at the same time.

You can put an advert in the local paper and ask if anyone is depressed and would like to share company on a walk, and perhaps you could start a club of walkers and help others in the process of getting better too, maybe someone out there shares your fate too.

With exercise in mind, if you have the mind for it, get fit, join a gym or just workout at home, or even better, in the park and back to nature again... getting fit, will encourage endorphins and you will look and feel automatically better.

Music is another way to feel good, but stay away from old songs that may remind you of certain times... move forward with new music and learn to sing, maybe even join a group or do karaoke.

Take up different sports, play football with friends... it's free! Take up tennis, golf, badminton, squash, cricket, yoga, Pilates, swimming, ice hockey, netball, playing cards, chess, Tiddly Winks, board games, sky-diving, snorkelling, throwing a Frisbee in the park.. Martial Arts, painting, take a course, take a diploma...(write a book) the list is endless and you have no reason not to want to be better and better every day in every way.

Bottom line, I do not want you to get back on track,...far from it...you may feel you might fall back to where you were before and we don't want that. So don't get back on track, instead be a different person, be a new person with a new start in life... someone who has a new purpose in your own life and give thanks that your maker has given you the hope and faith that brought you to this point in time. Your time, Your choices, Your life. Your life filled with love joy and happiness.

Round 11 to come next and nearly there.

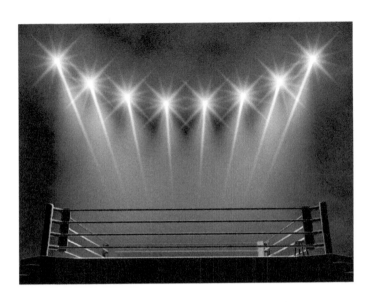

Out of the dark: Round 11
The Main Event

Well you have managed to weather the storm and made it to the penultimate round, so there is still the ability to fight, even after all you have been through in your life… and it will all be worth it in the end!

Whilst every round in the fight does not last a long time, this round will be one of the longest for obvious reasons.

I will attempt to re-capture elements of previous rounds to keep the flow of what you are going through and what you have endured and this round should see you in a better place mentally. You would have learned some fundamental coping mechanisms to allow you to function much better on a day to day basis.

So where to begin and that's where I wish to take you, to the beginning of your life, in fact before you even came into this world, where you were in your mother's womb and had no reference to what lay ahead, at this point you had the comfort and nurturing of a loving mother that kept you fed and safe. The day of your birth when you first came out of your mother's womb, you had no reference of the outside world, in fact all you had were your senses and feelings. These are vital instincts for what lay ahead.

There is no reference prior to any new event happening and you will only work with your senses and feelings.

So what do you feel when you're first born? You'll feel and sense some of the following:-

Light... smell... hot... cold... pain... hunger... sound ...oxygen ...etc., etc., and now you will have your first reference to work with.

Just for the record... **you were not born with depression!** But reference from life has given you this condition and it anchored itself within your psyche and made an imprint in your brain. Therefore we at least know that what we can install as a negative reference can be erased and replaced with a positive reference. This in turn will anchor a new reference. Positive and Negative are real thoughts and real energies. When the battery in a torch is pointing to the positive end and the other to the negative, the light will beam out. When you have a car battery with a positive and negative terminal, if you cross them the wrong way your car won't start and you could get a nasty shock. If you are feeling negative and low, you will omit a <u>negative pheromone</u> and this will go out to anyone in your transmitting zone and you will repel them, equally if you are being positive and feeling upbeat, then you will omit a <u>positive pheromone</u> and people and situations will be drawn toward you, just like two ends of a magnet, one will repel and the other will attract!

So our senses are vital for our gut feelings and survival and we need to work on how we transmit the right frequency!

Now about being SENSITIVE, our senses are there to protect us but sometimes we can be TOO sensitive and things will hurt us. You may have noticed that people who are rude, arrogant, mean and hard nosed, don't tend to get depressed, because they don't care about anyone or anything and have virtually no good feelings, therefore are not sensitive, whereas, if you suffer from depression, the chances are that you are a caring individual and do care and that you are sensitive to other peoples feelings and are probably quite spiritual even if you don't know it.

You probably are the one in the crowd to let the old lady go across the crossing or help someone get to the other side of the road or come to someone's rescue, or even help others when they are down, even though you are more down than they are… it's because you care, you are good and you have feelings, you could even be a mini councillor, so thank your lucky stars you have depression and know you are not an arsehole..!!

I for one always want to help people and if there is a God and a place called heaven and hell, I know he will be proud of me and what I do unselfishly for people and the planet, and on the day of reckoning I should have my ticket booked for the place above and not below. Where is yours booked for? It's never too late to be make that positive change, so the sooner the better.

So take some gratitude for being a good, kind and caring person and be grateful you were given depression! So you know for sure that you have a heart and have love within you.

The pressure of life

I hit on my own downfalls in my life in an earlier round but in fairness I only told you a small part of the absolute horrific pain I have endured throughout my life and there are no words to describe the continuous heartache and pain I have been bombarded with but I felt it better not to share this with you... otherwise by telling you, I believe you would have felt more down and that may have pushed you over the edge. Equally this is not actually about me, it's about you, and with all the terrible consistent pain I have encountered throughout my life, I now see it as all worthwhile, as it has allowed me to have an effect on so many lives in a positive fashion and am very grateful that I can make a positive difference in your life and maybe the butterfly effect will make you help another poor soul feel better.

Homework on your opponent

When going into the fight of your life its important to know your opponent, all their strengths and weaknesses. This to us is the enemy and the enemy in your case is depression. Once you have identified its strengths and weaknesses, you will have a far better chance of beating the enemy. So when and where best suits you? There is a saying, 'And these things shall come to pass' and I know that there were times when I felt dreadful when it hits and then the feeling eventually passes. When this feeling passes, it's then that you need to act! You can't say, "come on depression, hit me"... it just happens when it happens. You can't say to anxiety, "hit me"... it just happens when it happens. So use this valuable time when you have respite and explore its sensations and weaknesses, so when it strikes again you are more prepared and know that once again the feeling will pass.. So either brave it out, distract yourself or lock yourself away somewhere safe until the storm passes… remember, these are coping mechanisms and your own way to master your own emotions.

Blood Pressure

I suffered from high blood pressure… places and anticipation of seeing someone, or meeting, would bring it on.

Through certain meditation natural remedies like Hawthorn to regulate blood and heart and Passiflora for nervous system and anxiety. As a result of adopting these simple technics and remedies (not man made products), I no longer suffer from blood pressure at all.

Lets take a good example of a fight. We all know the famous film ROCKY and how a low-life bum, from nowhere with a measly existence, dug himself out of the gutter to become boxing champion of the world! When he was preparing for his fight against Apollo Creed, already world champion, he did not have the pedigree to take on such a mammoth opponent and yet his inner belief and inner desire got him to that fight, only knowing he wanted to be better, be special, not be beaten and not to disappear into the night!

Instead he knew he had the fight of his life on his hands and was going to get bloody and battered! Yet, ironically this was his strategy! You see, Rocky had been battered all his life, so one more kicking was not going to change much and this was his tactic… as he knew his only way to beat the champ was to let himself be used as a human punch bag and let the champ burn himself out.. Then when he had taken all that life had to hit him with, sorry, I meant Apollo had to hit him with... and with 'everything but the kitchen sink', he then dug deep inside his soul and not with strength but with deep desire, found the strength to over-power the champ and beat the crap out of him, to become the new, undisputed champion of the world!

So Mr or Mrs Balboa, are you ready to get your hands dirty and fight your enemy to gain what is rightfully yours? Or are you a bum and a loser? I can train you for the fight but I can't fight your wars for you… So dig deep and make me proud.

The Butterfly effect

Most of us have heard of the butterfly effect, but do we fully understand what this really means?

Through the power of thought, we can make something very small indeed and create something very big indeed.

In August 2014, I was sitting outside where I lived and was feeling so low and so lonely… I looked up to the sky and asked, God and the Universe please send me a sign to let me know what I should be doing in life and where should I be going. Nothing happened and I just kept my face in the sun, a few minutes later a stunning multi-coloured butterfly landed right next to me and sat looking at me with its little antenna flickering. I asked if I could take a photo of it with my Blackberry phone and luckily it did not object...it allowed me to get right up close and take the photo within a inch of it. I thanked the butterfly and then it just flew away. I didn't think anymore about it.

Later that year one of the ladies I know who is quite spiritual, mentioned she went to a craft fare and while she was there she met a young chap who was a medium and was giving readings for people passing through the fare. She said that he gave her a reading and she was most impressed and felt that I would benefit by seeing him.. I was slightly sceptical but as I was in need of help and guidance, I felt what did I have to lose. It took me a month to pluck up the courage to call him and he sounded like a nice down to earth chap, so I asked if I could come along the following week. When I met him I was quite surprised, as he was just an ordinary man and seemed to be both pleasant and caring. I didn't tell him anything, as I didn't want to give him any clues as to what was going on in my life or rather what was not going on in my life. He paused for a while and then started to point out that both my mother and father were no longer alive and that they were both here in spirit and have been looking out for me. He mentioned that my mother said not to drink the water where I live as it was effecting my immune system and adding to my depression, What the medium did not know is that where I lived the house was built on a site where there was a factory and it dumped Bromide into the ground and this in turn was affecting the water and from the day I moved in, I felt unwell and extremely depressed. He went on to say that your mum is saying buy bottled spring water and after a while you will improve. On another matter, being single at that point, I used to look on a dating site for someone that I could possibly date but was too low and I think they sensed it. However, he mentioned that your mum has also said that you need to go back on the dating site as you will be meeting someone on there in the new year. What I didn't understand is, how did the medium know any of this, as he was so accurate, I took his advice and went back on the site within a week or so. In January 2015, I was contacted by a lady on there and we appeared to have a synergy between us and with her kind help and inspiration, she encouraged me to finally start writing my book that had been only a vision 20 years prior!

We built up a wonderful rapport and spoke virtually every day. What was odd, is that she lived in America and I was not sure what the future may hold for us but week by week, she helped inspire me to write the book that YOU are now reading and played an important role in keeping me focused on writing. I wrote 11 chapters in 3 months.

We did finally meet, but sadly the chemistry was not there but felt she came into my life at the right time to inspire what you see now. I will always be so very grateful to her and only wish that there could have been a future together, but sometimes people come into your life for a reason and go out of your life for a reason and we are all on our own individual journeys.

The fact that the sequel of events that brought us to this point in time and place, construed to get this book out there and hopefully change lives for the positive and for that I give thanks to my mother for coming through at a time in need and for the special friend in America for being such a wonderful lady and I will never forget her.

The bottom line is... Out of the dark came the seed of an idea that became reality and pray this message and guidance will inspire you enough to give you back the life you so deserve and I send you sincere love and positive energy to help you mend and inspire others via the butterfly effect...x

Here is the photo that I took of the butterfly

Out of the Dark: Round 12
Going that Extra Mile!

As I start this day, I have had a restless night and had to get up at 5am, purely because thoughts have come into my mind from out there and felt I should share them with you.

We are all on our own individual journeys, yet feel we all share the same fate and destiny. Searching for answers, and wanting to know what we are doing here?

To think about where we are going, we sometimes have to go back to the beginning and try to understand what lessons or messages we were given a long time ago.

This is not so much an auto-biography, by contrast it's my reference as to how I am able to help you in your difficult and painful times.

I cast my mind back to when I was a child, around 6 years old… I had no brothers but 6 sisters, 3 older and 3 younger, so I was piggy in the middle… We had a loving mother who was an angel in her own right and owe much to this special lady and she is still helping from the spiritual world.. On the flip side, as you are aware, I had a dad who was a tyrant and used to beat me up on a regular basis, along with hitting my 6 sisters also.

I never new the love of a father, only that I spent my entire youth in fear and swore to myself that I would be a good father and not put my children through this torture.

Many years later and after my father's death and seeing a few clairvoyants, they all came up with the same comments… they said your dad is so sorry for the hell he put you through and has asked for your forgiveness, and as forgiveness is a major part of healing our-selves, I agreed to forgive him. Now in return he is now helping me from the other side and making up for all the wrong he did in this life. So you see, we are all on a journey, even after we leave the earthly plane.

Along with that journey, when I lost my business, home, furniture, cars, went through bankruptcy, etc., and my wife left me to bring up our children on my own, I knew I had a task ahead of me and wanted to do the best I could as a dad. Along with their schooling and caring for them and now being both mum and dad, I taught them to cook, iron, sew and clean and to be respectful.

My son, who is not just a son to me, but also a friend and a boy to be proud of, got married last year to a wonderful girl and it was a grand affair. A few months after the wedding, he took me for dinner and whilst we were at that dinner, he made a comment which really touched me, he said that when he has children of his own, he wanted to bring them up exactly how I brought him up and I was deeply touched, however, I did point out that I had a terrible childhood and my dad used to beat me up on a regular basis and had a miserable time… his reply was, yes but that has made you the man you are today and you have turned a bad thing into a good thing and you have became much stronger and a better person as a result! This meant a great deal to me.

My son's mother has not seen him for over 17 years and this must be terrible for any child for his mother to desert him and clearly she was not invited to his wedding. Yet he has turned out to be a special person, and I know every parent should love their child, but my love for him is far greater than just ordinary love and I will always be with him, in this life and even in spirit... He is my golden child.

So you see, we can look at the bad and blame that for how we have turned out or we can look at the lessons that were given and with free will, we can change our future for what we want and not allow ourselves to be controlled by wrong thinking and past events that cloud our judgment!

All that we think, say and do, is a reflection on who we are, therefore WE have control over our thoughts and the outcome and cannot blame or expect anyone else to live our lives for us.

With this in mind, I was guided to take up Alexander Technique many years ago and studied for around 6 years under a great teacher. I learned quickly and before long was working on him and his students. One day my teacher said to me that today you are going to work on Michael. Not knowing who Michael was, I said yeah no problem. When Michael turned up, I was a bit taken aback, as Michael was slightly retarded and was not sure what to do. My teacher told him that today Simon is going to work on you Michael, and with that Michael seemed a bit shocked and I was still not sure what to do. At that point I said to Michael, I am really tired today Michael and how about you work on me... with this Michael seemed even more surprised but made an effort to work on me. Whilst he was trying to work on me, I felt this was therapy for him too.

I then felt compelled to give him a big sincere hug and took him in my arms and gave him a real big caring hug. At that very moment, Michael put his head on my shoulder and seemed to be totally at ease and at peace, my teacher observed this and said, Michael, what do you feel? His reply in a soft voice was, LOVE. With that we all shared a tear and it sent a message to my brain.

Not quite understanding what just took place, when Michael left, my teacher said to me, did you know you're a healer and I replied "what me?" He said "yes and it was clear what you did with Michael and you should try to develop this gift." I did not really take him seriously and basically forgot it as quickly as it was said.

A number of years later my teacher was taken to hospital and was diagnosed with cancer of the prostate and I was extremely sad. This became very severe, to the point that one day I was called to the hospital by his wife and she told me he was dying and I was to come quickly.

When I arrived at the hospital I went to the ward where I could see him in a bed near the end and his family were around him. He had an oxygen mask on and was virtually white with no life left in him anymore and felt these were is last hours. I was not sure what my emotions were telling me at this point but felt that this man who had taken me under his wing, been a mentor, a friend and in many ways the loving father I never had... I felt something very special at that precise moment and when he put his hand out to say goodbye to me, I said to him with confidence in my words, "Do you know the good thing about being ill?" He replied "No!" I said "Getting better!" And with that, I took his hand and said, we are going to get better and just trust me, after all, it was you that told me I'm a healer. His

63

eyes then focused on mine, and all I could think about was the unconditional love I had for this wonderful man, and started to give positive energy and love to him. With creative visualisation, I saw him well and healthy and he started gaining faith and belief. I visualised every cell in his body alive and healthy, and the corrupt cells fall away like unwanted dust. After an hour I saw him getting colour back in his face and then he was able to talk and was conversing with me. After giving him unconditional love and healing, a few hours later he was sitting up and smiling. He went from being bed bound to walking up and down the ward and not understanding what occurred, they released him the following day and he went home.

As a form of recognition and gratitude, he decided to send a letter out to all of his students telling them about me and how I healed him and I was very proud for what I had achieved, yet still not understanding how this all works.

My aim from a young child was to help heal the world and just maybe via this book I can reach as many people as need that help and hopefully you are a part of that special journey.

This story is not to impress you, but to impress upon you, that with the right positive intention and love in your heart, **that we all can perform miracles.**

So we are now at the **end** or the **beginning** if you want to be positive?

So what is depression?

Depression is a feeling... for us to overcome depression we must first **own it**, yes **own it** and then and only then can we control it. By this process we can now master our feelings towards it. We have established that we are both caring and sensitive to the world around us and we know that we are not mean or nasty people, by contrast, we are good, kind and sensitive… so now we can turn **depression** into **impression** and **impress** to our **sensitivity** that we have **positivity** and true **purpose** finally.

So to summarise, you have managed to wade through the quagmire of despair, which you dug deep into the depths of your being, and have found your purpose… as a result of this, you have HELPED ME TO HELP YOU, TO HELP THE WORLD HELP EACH OTHER and you would have created the BUTTERFLY EFFECT!!!!

So with love in your heart, positivity in your head and belief in yourself, You have changed your destiny and now will get better and better, every day in every way!

Reality

You should now be more realistic about what is doable and with the coping mechanisms you now have in place. You do not need to be 100%... by contrast 60-80% would be more than sufficient for you to be able to control your mind and mood and start to enjoy peace and happiness in your life. Ignore the down days, which will be fewer, and fully exploit the good days and anchor the pattern.

Well done you, keep focused and keep up the positive momentum.

12 Day Re-Program Self-Help Section

This section is what helped me out of depression and it is my true belief that if you follow the simple techniques, take the natural remedies and adopt the coping mechanisms that I have designed, then all these should help you overcome your depression or at least improve things to a better level.

Bearing in mind, I am not a doctor prescribing medicine, purely someone who has been in health most of my life and with a diploma in Optimum Diet & Nutrition and in turn this helps me to help you.

There is also a simple 12 day log and this has been designed so you can utilise it to plot a 12 day re-program or modify to make it longer if you prefer, say 24 day program or a 48 day program and at the end of each cycle, simply by entering a figure of percentage level of how you feel day by day and week by week, then complete the life graph accordingly.

On the basis you wish to utilise this program, then it is advisable to order your natural remedies first and start taking these from the outset to get the best results. The remedies can be purchased from any good health store or if you prefer there is a link on the Out of the Dark website that can direct you to an online store where I purchased my products and I have arranged that readers of the book will qualify for a loyalty discount on their products. The list of products can be found after this section.

Please note, that assuming you wish to utilise this 12 day re-program, then it is strongly advisable to dedicate a day at a time for each section, as there will be a technique called EFT Tapping which should be carried out, and a simple meditation each day, and over the twelve day period this should improve your state of mind... the link to these can be found on the Out of the Dark website.

Equally there is a saying, ' Repetition is the basis of mother skill', so you may wish to read chapter one again and then complete the log, right through to chapter 12! It might be fair to say that when you first started reading there may have been some degree of doubt or hesitancy and by going back to the beginning and reviewing each round, this should have a more heightened effect and bring better results. You should pick up something you missed the first time round or be reading in a more positive frame of mind. So when you are ready tomorrow, please complete the second stage of the program by starting again at Round 1, thus making it now a 24 day program and where you may personally feel that you need further input and inspiration you can obviously read as many times as you so desire, or refer back to sections that are particular to you.

All this worked for me and I feel it should work for you too.. I would love to hear of your progress and you can make any comments to the forum on my website www.outofthedark.online

Best wishes

Simon

So here are a few things to get you to change (planet you)

Firstly, there are a few natural remedies that I would suggest you start taking:

5 HTP: helps alleviate stress and anxiety, also may help you sleep better.

Vitamin B12: helps alleviate stress.

DAMe: helps relieve depression and stress related blues.

L-Tyrosine: helps with anxiety and depression.

Total Calm Advanced: Helps with reducing the feelings of anxiety and panic with a calming effect on the system

Therapies

There are endless therapies that are out there and you have no excuses for not trying
the ones that work for you…

EFT Tapping (Emotional freedom technique) is a good start, (Ahhh… but what's this going to cost me you might say) and the answer is you either go to a EFT therapist and pay or you go onto an EFT tapping site and copy what they tell you for FREE. These work on your sensory points and there are many different EFT therapist online that offer instruction of how to do this easy tapping on yourself.. I did it and it helped me.

Hypnotherapy If you have the disposable cash, then other therapies like Hypnotherapy can certainly help to change the way you think and you may need to try a few different therapists to find the one that works for you. Try to remember, you must be realistic, you are not expecting a100% change from these different therapies, only small positive changes that exponentially will make your life graph work.

I had 3 Hypnotherapy treatments and it made a percentage positive difference in me, so it should offer a helpful change for you too.

Reflexology is another good one. It works on the acupressure points in your feet and will help stimulate your meridians in your body. This will help increase your state of well-being, and help with ailments in your system. It also helps alleviate stress and will certainly help with depression. I go once a month for my session without fail.

Healing like Reiki or other forms of healing are certainly high on the list for helping depression and I would strongly recommend healing as a positive way to getting a lot of negative energy out of you and allow you to relax in the process. I have had many healing sessions and they made a big difference to my mood straight after. In return, I now offer healing to other poor souls. You can find a non-denominational spiritual church or hall for healing and words of comfort.

Massage is another way to release stress and to get that feel good factor, bearing in mind this will help move toxins out of your body and once again, this is 'you' time and will allow you to de-stress and find some enjoyment in someone caring for your body. I have a massage once a week.

Alexander Technique is another good way to relax and de-stress and also to learn about posture and the body. It helps to re-align the body and help it function more efficiently. I studied Alexander Technique for 6 years and combine this with my teachings.

Emo Trance
Emo Trance is an energy healing modality, which actually goes beyond healing. It helps take you through the negative energy and helps to restore your positive state. Once again you can get more information online and if you require a practitioner you can email us.

Theta Healing
Theta Healing is a meditative technique while the client and practitioner are in a Theta Brainwave state - an altered consciousness where brainwaves are slowed to a relaxed mode.

Action Plan
Firstly, it is strongly recommended that directly after this chapter, you order the remedies suggested above. These are all natural and should not interfere with any other medication, however you are welcome to consult your doctor prior should you so desire.

With regards to the techniques that are recommended above, one of the main techniques that I would recommend that should form part of your daily routine should be the EFT tapping technique.

The remedies and the EFT tapping Youtube link can be accessed or ordered via the Out of the Dark website listed below:

www.outofthedark.online

Using the website link above, it is advised that you follow the link to access the EFT tapping which is totally free. In addition to this, there will be a link to one of the 4 simple meditations that are also provided by myself free of charge.

The EFT tapping video will be easy to follow and the meditations provided will be self-explanatory and all you have to do is sit back and go for the ride.

After you have completed the EFT tapping, please access and carry out the Day 1 meditation, which has been specifically designed for this Round.

So in reality, you can't control the past but you can shape your future x

Additions

Immune System

Along with taking the right supplements to help your mood, it's important to stay away from products that affect your immune system like deodorants with harmful chemicals like aluminium etc. This will apply to many things like toothpaste, perfume and aftershaves, washing up liquids, soaps etc.

If you don't know where to go to get any of these natural alternatives, just go to the Out of The Dark website for outlets stocking them www.outofthedark.online

Stones and Crystals

For centuries Stones and Crystals have been used for their earthly energies and different types are used for different effects...bearing in mind, these are all natural elements from mother earth and are here for your benefit for each of our individual circumstances.

Firstly, I would recommend **Aquamarine**, this light blue stone is known to offer soothing, pacify nerves and banish phobias whilst ensuring calm and tranquility.

Second, **Ammetrine**, the entwined power of Amethyst and Citrine, makes this a unique stone, believed to be an exceptional cleanser and energiser.

Third, **Hematite**, enhances personal magnetism, will and courage. Believed beneficial for blood, stress and nerves.

Fourth, **Rose Quartz,** known as the love stone, aids peacefulness and calm in relationships, and is said to ease stress and tension and assist in sleep.

Last but no least, **Amber**, this stone is a must for balancing mind and emotions... releasing negative energy, it aids in manifestation, eases stress and clearing phobias and fears. If possible, try to get a necklace so that you can wear this stone, so you always have protection.

As all these stones and crystals are of the earth, they will need to be cleansed every day after wearing, to get rid of the negativity and where possible use rain water to cleanse and to re-charge, place on the ground, preferably in earth and with access to moon-light or sun-light.

You can get a pouch to carry around during the day for protection and at the side of your bed at night when you sleep.

You may wish to thank the stones for their help, they are mineral just like you and it's an exchange of energy

A Brief introduction into Meditation

Welcome to this brief intro into meditation. There are many forms of meditation and many views on how to carry out. After doing meditation for some time now, this is my own version of how I feel it will best help you...

Firstly, the object of the exercise is to get you into a relaxed frame of mind in a safe environment, by carrying out some simple steps to enable you to feel both at peace and in control of your emotions. If you are advanced in meditation, then a lot of this you will already know, however we are going to assume you are new to meditation and I will gently guide you through some basics to get you started.

For the purpose of this self help book, the meditations will be kept relatively short, some slightly longer than the others but to give you time to adjust and to get into the swing of things.

To start with, you will need to practice in a safe environment and not driving a car or carrying out any work or tasks, your phone switched off and as quiet an environment as possible. Give yourself 10 minutes or so to be able to switch off from the outside world and take some time out.

Ideally sit in a comfortable chair, if you have ear phones that would be best or simply listen from a lap top, etc.... Follow the guided meditation that you can listen to on the 'Out of the Dark' website... there are 4 different meditations, you can alternate. You don't need to download anything, just follow the link and listen.

When you listen to them, preferably don't fall asleep, as you will miss the message and it won't have the desired effect. If you carry it out correctly, you should fall into a conscious trance, allowing you to come back at any time you desire, but you will be guided when to start and finish.

For the best part, you will be aware of your calm and elongated breathing, centering yourself and learning to control your mind and emotions. All this is achievable, with the will to want to get better and trust in yourself....The rest is purely a process.. As time goes by and with enough easy practice, you will see yourself getting better and better, every day in every way...

I think it only fair to say, a lot of work as gone into compiling these meditations and there is no charge whatsoever to you... they are created and given with love, so please enjoy and I will be with you every step of the way.

Now please access and carry out the Day 1 meditation found on the website which has been specifically designed for this Round.

Now we come to the Daily Log entries:

Daily summary log Round 1
A-Bout Depression

Here is an opportunity to carry out the same process that I adopted and it worked for me. I think it fair to say, that all of the remedies, therapies, and coping mechanisms mentioned are all of the disciplines that I carried out and they worked for me, helping me get out of depression and I feel that many of these will work for you too, so please give it your best shot and dedicate yourself to the program.

As this will be your first log, there are a few simple things to get you started:-

Firstly, either read round 1 again or view the summary below.

Second, carry out the EFT tapping via the website link.

Third, there is an intro into meditation if you are a beginner and a short meditation, if you are more advanced, then there are 3 others you can choose from or use whatever material that you feel comfortable with.

Bearing in mind that to start this log, it is advisable to already have started the natural health remedies so they can be working in your system during this process.

Here is a reminder of round 1.

In brief, this section deals with losing virtually everything, abuse of most kinds, suffering from panic attacks, blood pressure, not being able to look people in the eye, not being able to go out of the house, not being able to drive on the motorway, heavy depression and wanting to basically give up.

On the flip side, knowing there is something that keeps driving us on, a certain faith we hang onto, understanding that everything happens for a reason and life is about personal growth and ultimately, Purpose!

Once you have refreshed your thoughts on the chapter, carried out the EFT tapping and the meditation, then please complete the daily log overleaf...

Each round should be different and to help you improve, we need to introduce other therapies and techniques to help you to re- program your mind and thoughts to a more realistic state!

Round 1 End of Chapter ...Personal Daily Log

In order to monitor and aid your level of improvement, it would be worthwhile registering your level of progress, and be as honest as you possibly can and how it made you feel, then relay your thoughts below accordingly.

On a scale of 1 to 100 we need to register the percentage level of how you feel, with 1 being very bad and 100 being very good.

1. What is your level after reading this round?   ....

2. List <u>one</u> negative factor you will eliminate to improve your mental state today:

....

3. List <u>one</u> positive step you will take to improve your mental state today:

....

That is all we need to register for today and thanks for being true to you!

Taking back your power

Its much easier to find fault or negativity in aspects in our daily lives but it takes real strength and determination to see the positive in any given situation, so with that in mind, a good way to take back your power is to list all the positive things that you did the day before and list them down on this page as a statement that you are taking positive things with you into the future. By contrast, anything bad or negative that happened the day before, you simply dismiss and leave it in the past where it belongs. So today list all the good things that happened yesterday :)

....
....
....

....
....
....

....
....
....

Daily summary log Round 2
Digging Deep

Moving forward, we need to complete the round 2 log by carrying out the EFT tapping and the meditation that can be found via the Out of the Dark website and read round 2 again or refresh your thoughts with the round summary below.

Needless to say, the EFT tapping that has been suggested is the main one that helped me but you can search others online and may find it helpful to vary different guides for this. Equally, the meditation that I have designed, you may wish to try alternative meditations and therefore you can always scan online for others you may prefer but be careful to use those that are specific for helping lift you out of depression and making a calming influence on you mind.

Here is a reminder of the content of round 2

In the round we look at not over stepping the mark with trying to get too much too soon and being realistic with your goals. It's understanding that negativity is stronger than positivity and you will have to work hard at being more positive.

Try to find the good in most things and ignore the bad. Use pain to gain, in other words, let pain be the leverage you need to inspire you to get out of the quick sand you are in and swim free.

Once you have refreshed your memory of round 2 and carried out the EFT tapping and meditation, then please complete the log overleaf.

At this point I would now like you to introduce other therapies into your life from the many suggested here. We need to vary these techniques to aid our improvement and to broaden our scope. Bearing in mind, not all of these are free like the EFT tapping. So money permitting, try to source some alternative therapies round by round and log by log.

All or most of the therapies that are listed, I have tried myself and that is why I can recommend to you, not all are free and some you may need to go to see a therapist and pay but I feel its a small price to pay to get your life back. In some cases you doctor may be able to refer you to therapies like CBT etc, so you don't have to pay. The four main ones I would firstly recommend are the EFT tapping, Emo Trance, Theta and hypnotherapy, the others are supplement to these.

The meditation is a must for every day.

Round 2 End of Chapter Personal Daily Log

In order to monitor and aid your level of improvement, it would be worthwhile registering your level of progress, and be as honest as you possibly can and how it made you feel, then relay your thoughts below accordingly.

On a scale of 1 to 100 we need to register the percentage level of how you feel, with 1 being very bad and 100 being very good.

1. What is your level after reading this round? ....

2. List <u>one</u> negative factor you will eliminate to improve your mental state today:

....

3. List <u>one</u> positive step you will take to improve your mental state today:

....

That is all we need to register for today and thanks for being true to you!

Taking back your power

Its much easier to find fault or negativity in aspects in our daily lives but it takes real strength and determination to see the positive in any given situation, so with that in mind, a good way to take back your power is to list all the positive things that you did the day before and list them down on this page as a statement that you are taking positive things with you into the future. By contrast, anything bad or negative that happened the day before, you simply dismiss and leave it in the past where it belongs. So today list all the good things that happened yesterday :)

....
....
....

....
....
....

....
....
....

Daily summary log round 3
Keeping your defences up!

This should be day 3, especially on the basis you are allowing a day's break for each log entry.

So now we need to carry out the main disciplines, meditation, EFT tapping or alternative therapies being introduced and refreshing our thoughts for the round 3 log entry, for which the reminder follows here.

Here is the reminder for round 3

Creative visualisation is a must and see yourself creating the life you want, this along with positive affirmations will strengthen your vision.

Belief in a higher force and sincere prayer is all about reaching out and trusting your faith.

We all need something to believe in and this becomes more prevalent when you are lost in the wilderness and need help and guidance.

Please complete the daily log and stay strong on your journey.

Round 3 End of Chapter Personal Daily Log

In order to monitor and aid your level of improvement, it would be worthwhile registering your level of progress, and be as honest as you possibly can and how it made you feel, then relay your thoughts below accordingly.

On a scale of 1 to 100 we need to register the percentage level of how you feel, with 1 being very bad and 100 being very good.

1. What is your level after reading this round? ………

2. List <u>one</u> negative factor you will eliminate to improve your mental state today:

………………………………………………………………………

3. List <u>one</u> positive step you will take to improve your mental state today:

………………………………………………………………………

That is all we need to register for today and thanks for being true to you!

Taking back your power

Its much easier to find fault or negativity in aspects in our daily lives but it takes real strength and determination to see the positive in any given situation, so with that in mind, a good way to take back your power is to list all the positive things that you did the day before and list them down on this page as a statement that you are taking positive things with you into the future. By contrast, anything bad or negative that happened the day before, you simply dismiss and leave it in the past where it belongs. So today list all the good things that happened yesterday :)

....
....
....

....
....
....

....
....
....

Daily summary log Round 4 –
A Star in the Making

Here we are on day four of our daily summary log and by now you should be into the swing of things.

So carry out the therapy that you have decided upon, most days I did the EFT tapping and some days I did more than one therapy, as I was committed to getting better asap. The meditation is a must every day and I advanced to twice a day, so you may wish to expand on this as you feel necessary and then either read or refresh your memory for this round.

Round 4 reminder

In this round we looked at the power of right thinking and the wonders of the universe, where we all ultimately came from! How everything in the universe is connected and we are most definitely a part of its dynamic flow. Where everything has purpose and you are a very special part of the master plan.

Please now complete your daily log and may the force be with you :)

Round 4 End of Chapter Personal Daily Log

In order to monitor and aid your level of improvement, it would be worthwhile registering your level of progress, and be as honest as you possibly can and how it made you feel, then relay your thoughts below accordingly.

On a scale of 1 to 100 we need to register the percentage level of how you feel, with 1 being very bad and 100 being very good.

1. What is your level after reading this round? ………

2. List <u>one</u> negative factor you will eliminate to improve your mental state today:

……………………………………………………………………

3. List <u>one</u> positive step you will take to improve your mental state today:

……………………………………………………………………

That is all we need to register for today and thanks for being true to you!

Taking back your power

Its much easier to find fault or negativity in aspects in our daily lives but it takes real strength and determination to see the positive in any given situation, so with that in mind, a good way to take back your power is to list all the positive things that you did the day before and list them down on this page as a statement that you are taking positive things with you into the future. By contrast, anything bad or negative that happened the day before, you simply dismiss and leave it in the past where it belongs. So today list all the good things that happened yesterday :)

....
....
....

....
....
....

....
....
....

Daily summary log round 5
Throwing in the Towel

Here we are on day five and building some progressive momentum, also getting accustomed to the process that we need to build on.

Whilst we need to introduce new forms of therapies, as this will enhance our chances of overall improvement, I still carried out both the EFT tapping and always the meditation, as this helped compound the daily effect. So it's entirely up to you how you differentiate these therapies, I can only say it worked for me.

Round 5 reminder

In this round I spoke about throwing in the towel, giving up, as this tends to be around when depression takes hold and this is the time to really dig deep. Either by going into hibernation during the spell of low or facing your demons head on and battling through, whichever you feel you can handle. This could be a good time for a therapy like massage or reflexology, which will be very therapeutic and quietly relaxing.

Please now complete your daily log and keep your faith

Round 5 End of Chapter Personal Daily Log

In order to monitor and aid your level of improvement, it would be worthwhile registering your level of progress, and be as honest as you possibly can and how it made you feel, then relay your thoughts below accordingly.

On a scale of 1 to 100 we need to register the percentage level of how you feel, with 1 being very bad and 100 being very good.

1. What is your level after reading this round? ....

2. List <u>one</u> negative factor you will eliminate to improve your mental state today:

....

3. List <u>one</u> positive step you will take to improve your mental state today:

....

That is all we need to register for today and thanks for being true to you!

Taking back your power

Its much easier to find fault or negativity in aspects in our daily lives but it takes real strength and determination to see the power is to list all the positive things that you did the day before and list them down on this page as a statement that positive in any given situation, so with that in mind, a good way to take back your you are taking positive things with you into the future. By contrast, anything bad or negative that happened the day before, you simply dismiss and leave it in the past where it belongs. So today list all the good things that happened yesterday :)

....
....
....

....
....
....

....
....
....

Daily summary log round 6
Half empty or Half Full

Here we are on day six of your daily summary log and now effectively half way through the 12 day re-program.

By now the remedies you have been taking should start to kick in and you will be getting induced levels of Serotonin and Dopamine to create those feel good factors in your brain.

I honestly believe that to fight the battle against depression, and subject to how heavy yours is, it will require different levels of support and the more good stuff that you feed into your system, then the greater chance you have to master your mind and emotions.

Round 6 reminder

Here we are at half empty or half full and we need to be realistic with our goals and not expect too much too soon. With this in mind, you don't need to be 100% better to feel good again but small improvements on a daily basis will exponentially give you a percentage increase that you can physically measure. So don't set yourself up for self sabotage by doing things or going to places that have a negative effect on you and stay with better energy. Remember to say positive affirmations to yourself and out to the Universe.

Please now complete your daily log and well done for getting past half way home:)

Round 6 End of Chapter Personal Daily Log

In order to monitor and aid your level of improvement, it would be worthwhile registering your level of progress, and be as honest as you possibly can and how it made you feel, then relay your thoughts below accordingly.

On a scale of 1 to 100 we need to register the percentage level of how you feel, with 1 being very bad and 100 being very good.

1. What is your level after reading this round? ....

2. List <u>one</u> negative factor you will eliminate to improve your mental state today:

....

3. List <u>one</u> positive step you will take to improve your mental state today:

....

That is all we need to register for today and thanks for being true to you!

Taking back your power

Its much easier to find fault or negativity in aspects in our daily lives but it takes real strength and determination to see the positive in any given situation, so with that in mind, a good way to take back your power is to list all the positive things that you did the day before and list them down on this page as a statement that you are taking positive things with you into the future. By contrast, anything bad or negative that happened the day before, you simply dismiss and leave it in the past where it belongs. So today list all the good things that happened yesterday :)

....
....
....

....
....
....

....
....
....

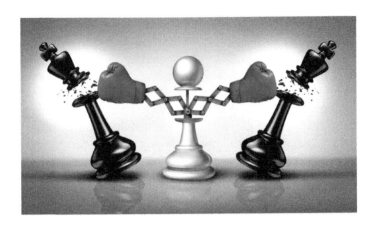

Daily summary log round 7
The Sucker Punch

So here we are past half way and building momentum. With the daily exercise for your brain, a combination of EFT tapping, meditation and alternative therapies, you will be re-programming how you think and feel. This in turn should give you more control over your mind and emotions.

Another element that we can introduce will be the coping mechanisms and these will help to stabilise your day to day reactions to places and situations. So think ahead of the activity and don't allow yourself to be compromised.

Here is a reminder of the content of round 7

Addictions such as booze, drugs, gambling etc, are all a downward spiral and sometimes difficult to shake off. These tend to be a form of crutch to lean on when we can't support our own mind and emotions, so get tough and take back your control. For this to happen you will probably need to substitute with something else, so join a gym, take up Pilates or yoga, play games, get a job in a garden centre, any distraction of this nature will help you through the quagmire and weather the storm.

Please now complete the daily log and keep up the good work.

Round 7 End of Chapter Personal Daily Log

In order to monitor and aid your level of improvement, it would be worthwhile registering your level of progress, and be as honest as you possibly can and how it made you feel, then relay your thoughts below accordingly.

On a scale of 1 to 100 we need to register the percentage level of how you feel, with 1 being very bad and 100 being very good.

1. What is your level after reading this round? ....

2. List <u>one</u> negative factor you will eliminate to improve your mental state today:

....

3. List <u>one</u> positive step you will take to improve your mental state today:

....

That is all we need to register for today and thanks for being true to you!

Taking back your power

Its much easier to find fault or negativity in aspects in our daily lives but it takes real strength and determination to see the positive in any given situation, so with that in mind, a good way to take back your power is to list all the positive things that you did the day before and list them down on this page as a statement that you are taking positive things with you into the future. By contrast, anything bad or negative that happened the day before, you simply dismiss and leave it in the past where it belongs. So today list all the good things that happened yesterday :)

....
....
....

....
....
....

....
....
....

Daily summary log round 8
You V Negativity

As we now move into round 8, we should be feeling the effects of the program and noticing some small changes in ourselves. At this point I could personally feel some positive gain and started to feel more in control and more relaxed with my daily routine. Its important to remember, Rome was not built in a day! It took you quite a while to get into the state of depression you are or were in and it will take some determined effort during this process to get the desired results. As mentioned, you can read the chapters again one by one or just recapture elements of the rounds by the reminders below.

Here is a reminder of the content of round 8

This chapter reflects on your belief system and when we are at our darkest hour, how we tend to cry out, 'God help me', this is either a knee jerk reaction or perhaps we feel deep in our soul and spirit that there is this higher force that governs all things.. I can only tell you that when I was at my all time low and I was struggling to go one step further, then and only then did my inner voice take over and cry out for help. Seeing the lady counsellor was extremely important but what came out of it was even more important, it allowed me to see the vision of bright white light that shone through that window and gave me the vision to write a book and it even gave me the title, 'Out of the Dark' by some sort of divine intervention and this is the book you are reading today! So there is always hope dear one :)

Please now complete the daily log overleaf and may God be with you.

Round 8 End of Chapter Personal Daily Log

In order to monitor and aid your level of improvement, it would be worthwhile registering your level of progress, and be as honest as you possibly can and how it made you feel, then relay your thoughts below accordingly.

On a scale of 1 to 100 we need to register the percentage level of how you feel, with 1 being very bad and 100 being very good.

1. What is your level after reading this round? ....

2. List <u>one</u> negative factor you will eliminate to improve your mental state today:

....

3. List <u>one</u> positive step you will take to improve your mental state today:

....

That is all we need to register for today and thanks for being true to you!

Taking back your power

Its much easier to find fault or negativity in aspects in our daily lives but it takes real strength and determination to see the positive in any given situation, so with that in mind, a good way to take back your power is to list all the positive things that you did the day before and list them down on this page as a statement that you are taking positive things with you into the future. By contrast, anything bad or negative that happened the day before, you simply dismiss and leave it in the past where it belongs. So today list all the good things that happened yesterday :)

....
....
....

....
....
....

....
....
....

Daily summary log round 9
A Good Corner Man

We are now 75% through the re-programming and should be quite fluent with how this all works now. Like any computer, a program can be created and deleted and what we are endeavouring to do is to eliminate the old pattern that had formed and replace with a new shiny up to date brand new you pattern.. Remember we program computers, they don't program us!

Don't see yourself how you used to be, low self esteem and lost in the wilderness, see yourself how you want to be, have that vision clear in your mind and be totally committed to your goal, it's your God given right to have a happy life and you 100% deserve it!!

Again, you are not requested to read round 9 over again but this is your choice and only you can decide how much input you want to absorb.

Here is a reminder of the content of round 9

Thoughts are things and what we think, say and do forms our environment and eventually our world, so be careful of what you think and try to create positive thoughts instead.

A good corner man essentially means someone looking out for your interest and it's always good to seek out some form of counselling, there is always someone ready to listen.

Emotions can ruin us and when we are low and vulnerable, the slightest thing can knock us off keel, so when you are doing anything in your daily routine, try to leave the letter E out of Emotion and just make it motion.

Please now complete the daily log overleaf and keep up the good momentum.

Round 9 End of Chapter Personal Daily Log

In order to monitor and aid your level of improvement, it would be worthwhile registering your level of progress, and be as honest as you possibly can and how it made you feel, then relay your thoughts below accordingly.

On a scale of 1 to 100 we need to register the percentage level of how you feel, with 1 being very bad and 100 being very good.

1. What is your level after reading this round? ....

2. List <u>one</u> negative factor you will eliminate to improve your mental state today:

....

3. List <u>one</u> positive step you will take to improve your mental state today:

....

That is all we need to register for today and thanks for being true to you!

Taking back your power

Its much easier to find fault or negativity in aspects in our daily lives but it takes real strength and determination to see the positive in any given situation, so with that in mind, a good way to take back your power is to list all the positive things that you did the day before and list them down on this page as a statement that you are taking positive things with you into the future. By contrast, anything bad or negative that happened the day before, you simply dismiss and leave it in the past where it belongs. So today list all the good things that happened yesterday :)

....
....
....

....
....
....

....
....
....

Daily summary log round 10
If you wanna win you have to Planet!

We now arrive at round 10 and on the home stretch. There are no short cuts with this stuff and we can't go around it, so we have to go through it! You should be feeling the positive effects of this plan and it definitely worked for me, in fact at this point I was feeling highly motivated and one of the main things I would recommend is that you try to enjoy the process and this should have a more compound effect.

Every day that passes is another day for the remedies to be working in your system and the more therapies you try and work with, the more positive input you will encounter. Not all of the therapies will suit you but there will be those that will and try to take all the good and ignore the rest.

It is definitely worth reading round 10 again but if you feel that you took in what was said, then here is a reminder of the main points:-

Firstly, does the Planet give you depression, well the answer should be No, as nature should be a part of our dynamic flow, so if the Planet does not give us depression, then people and situations are the problem, therefore be aware of people and places that have a negative draining effect on you and stay away! Find alternative people and places that leave you feeling lifted, instead of drained.

The Sun is an important part of our daily lives and without it we would cease to exist.. Try to catch the Sun's rays on your face everyday, even if its only for 20 seconds, your body and mind will feel positive charging elements that will create a feel good factor.

Please now complete the daily log overleaf and those smiley face emoticons are virtually always on a Sun background

....
....
....

....
....
....

....
....
....

Round 10 End of Chapter Personal Daily Log

In order to monitor and aid your level of improvement, it would be worthwhile registering your level of progress, and be as honest as you possibly can and how it made you feel, then relay your thoughts below accordingly.

On a scale of 1 to 100 we need to register the percentage level of how you feel, with 1 being very bad and 100 being very good.

1. What is your level after reading this round? ………

2. List <u>one</u> negative factor you will eliminate to improve your mental state today:

………………………………………………………………

3. List <u>one</u> positive step you will take to improve your mental state today:

………………………………………………………………

That is all we need to register for today and thanks for being true to you!

Taking back your power

Its much easier to find fault or negativity in aspects in our daily lives but it takes real strength and determination to see the positive in any given situation, so with that in mind, a good way to take back your power is to list all the positive things that you did the day before and list them down on this page as a statement that you are taking positive things with you into the future. By contrast, anything bad or negative that happened the day before, you simply dismiss and leave it in the past where it belongs. So today list all the good things that happened yesterday :)

....
....
....

....
....
....

....
....
....

Daily summary log round 11
The Main Event

Here we are at the penultimate round and you should be totally committed to wanting to feel good again. Nothing worthwhile comes easy and anything worthwhile is worth fighting for, hence the rounds of a fight and you are fighting for what is rightfully yours!

I knew deep down in the depths of my soul, that I did not want that creeping feeling of gloom, helplessness and suffocating to be part of me anymore and I would rather the pain of fighting through to success, than the pain of failure and was not prepared to be a victim anymore!

No one can have someone else's thoughts and no one can have your thoughts, we are responsible for what we think, say and do, as a result, We and only We can control our mind and emotions, so dig deep, take a deep breath and follow my lead!

Once again, I feel it important to read over this round again but if you are confident that you have taken in all that was said, then here is a brief reminder of the main points of round 11.

We were not born with depression and going back to the beginning is a good place to start.

Reference of Light, Smell, Hot, Cold, Pain, Hunger, Sound, etc are all feelings and it is for us to determine what all these senses mean to us and how we perceive them. There is a saying, 'it's not what people say and do to us, it's how we react to what people say and do to us', so with this in mind, try to stay focused on knowing that you must not get affected to the negative and not allow yourself to waver.

Remembering how Rocky was determined to become the undisputed boxing champion of the world and all those that said he was a bum and a loser just made him more determined to prove them all wrong and used that as leverage to drive him forward, ultimately to win!

Please now complete the daily log overleaf and fight for what is rightfully yours!

Round 11 End of Chapter Personal Daily Log

In order to monitor and aid your level of improvement, it would be worthwhile registering your level of progress, and be as honest as you possibly can and how it made you feel, then relay your thoughts below accordingly.

On a scale of 1 to 100 we need to register the percentage level of how you feel, with 1 being very bad and 100 being very good.

1. What is your level after reading this round? ………

2. List <u>one</u> negative factor you will eliminate to improve your mental state today:

………………………………………………………………

3. List <u>one</u> positive step you will take to improve your mental state today:

………………………………………………………………

That is all we need to register for today and thanks for being true to you!

Taking back your power

Its much easier to find fault or negativity in aspects in our daily lives but it takes real strength and determination to see the positive in any given situation, so with that in mind, a good way to take back your power is to list all the positive things that you did the day before and list them down on this page as a statement that you are taking positive things with you into the future. By contrast, anything bad or negative that happened the day before, you simply dismiss and leave it in the past where it belongs. So today list all the good things that happened yesterday :)

....
....
....

....
....
....

....
....
....

Daily summary log round 12
Going that extra Mile!

Well here we are at the last round and you should have accumulated some useful info to collate a measurable graph and that will assist you in identifying your level of improvement. I think it only fair to say that I managed to shake off depression within roughly three to four months and considering I had depression for three to four years, that was not bad going. The 12 day re-programme is what started me off on the right track and equally, the 12 days re-program became 24 days, 48 days and so on, until I was totally satisfied that I had shaken off this heavy feeling!

They say repetition is the basis of mother skill, so I would strongly suggest that you carry out the therapies, take the remedies and adopt the coping mechanisms as many times as you can to increase your chances of improvement. It's what worked for me and welcome you to do the same.

I feel it's all about having the right tools to do the job and hopefully I have given you the ammunition required to get the job done.

Here is a reminder of some relevant points for round 12. In brief, everything happens for a reason, good or bad and even when we think something is bad, we should still try to find the good in any given situation.. for example, even though I went through some horrific times in my life, it taught me valuable lessons and they say what doesn't kill you makes you great. I had faced great pain and sorrow and when I look back now, this was all preparation for what lay ahead, teaching me survival techniques, ultimately purpose, and that purpose was to help to be able to help you my good friend Out of the Dark!

Please now complete the last daily log and try to work out what is your purpose in life?

Round 12 End of Chapter Personal Daily Log

In order to monitor and aid your level of improvement, it would be worthwhile registering your level of progress, and be as honest as you possibly can and how it made you feel, then relay your thoughts below accordingly.

On a scale of 1 to 100 we need to register the percentage level of how you feel, with 1 being very bad and 100 being very good.
1. What is your level after reading this round? ....

2. List <u>one</u> negative factor you will eliminate to improve your mental state today:

....

3. List <u>one</u> positive step you will take to improve your mental state today:

....

That is all we need to register for today and thanks for being true to you!

Taking back your power

Its much easier to find fault or negativity in aspects in our daily lives but it takes real strength and determination to see the positive in any given situation, so with that in mind, a good way to take back your power is to list all the positive things that you did the day before and list them down on this page as a statement that you are taking positive things with you into the future. By contrast, anything bad or negative that happened the day before, you simply dismiss and leave it in the past where it belongs. So today list all the good things that happened yesterday :)

....
....
....

....
....
....

....
....
....

Life Graph

Now we arrive at the life graph and this should be relatively simple to complete.

There were three questions at the end of each Round and whilst they are all there for your daily reference, question no.1 asked what is your reading after reading this Round, and it is that which we will need to register on the graph overleaf... In the 12 sections of this graph, kindly place your reading that you registered in Round 1 on the graph in the first section, and likewise in the second section for Round 2, and so on until you have logged each entry right through to Round 12.

Now draw a continued line of reference from number one through all of the numbered entries until you get to number 12... If you have followed all of the techniques, taken the natural remedies and adopted the coping mechanisms given, then your graph should show an upward trend and plot your personal day to day improvement and this can be improved. If there are any dips in the graph then don't be despondent, as this can happen, but overall you should see an upward trend and this can improve with more positive commitment from you.

Just to recap, the health remedies will assist in increasing Dopamine levels in the brain, along with Serotonin and Oxytocin, which all go towards improving your mood and feel good factor. Regular exercise will help take your mind off problems and also induce the Endorphins in your body for a well being effect and a feeling of uplift. Then the Therapies suggested should improve your state of mind and encourage the Neurotransmitters in the brain to influence happier thoughts and start the re-programming effect... All this and more should assist you in your own personal progress

100%
98%
96%
94%
92%
90%
88%
86%
84%
82%
80%
78%
76%
74%
72%
70%
68%
64%
62%
60%
58%
56%
54%
52%
50%
48%
46%
44%
42%
40%
38%
36%
34%
32%
30%
28%
26%
24%
22%
20%
18%
16%
14%
12%
10%
8%
6%
4%
2%
0%

Round 1	Round 2	Round 3	Round 4	Round 5	Round 6	Round 7	Round 8	Round 9	Round 10	Round 11	Round 12

The life graph should assist you in monitoring your level of improvement that you have achieved and whilst you will not see 100% improvement, as this is virtually impossible, you should see a marked improvement which will be enough to get you on the right path, along with the coping mechanisms we have suggested. This will improve things exponentially and you can always read the book as many times as you wish, and revert back to certain sections that you feel will help further..

Well done you, keep focused and keep up the positive momentum.

Summary:

- Depression is a feeling
- Natural remedies
- Natural therapies
- Re-programming
- Power of prayer
- Creative visualization
- Counselling
- Your life purpose
- Your right to feel good
- Past references
- CD meditations
- Coping mechanisms
  like EFT tapping, hypnotherapy etc. ...

You now have all the ammunition to fight the war to change you for the better.

So in reality, you can't control the past but you can shape your future x

There is an old saying, "repetition is the basis of mother skill" and normally when depression is prevalent, reading or doing anything for the first time will incorporate a degree of doubt and fear. Needless to say, this may have been present when you first started this program. Therefore it is highly recommended that you complete the process for a second time as the program should have a more heightened effect and bring better results.

So when you are ready tomorrow, please complete the second stage of the program by starting again at Round 1, thus making it now a 24 day program and where you may personally feel that you need further input and inspiration particular to you.

Please bear in mind this is your self-help book and manual that you can call upon whenever you feel the need.

Well done and keep up the good work!

Disclaimer

This book has been compiled with a view to helping those poor souls in the dark and whilst every precaution has been taken when giving advice from the knowledge obtained, the author and anyone associated with the book cannot be held responsible for any reason whatsoever.

I trust this is purely a precaution and no one will have any reason to be dissatisfied and moreover, they should benefit from the love and effort that is offered to change a life for the better.

Author Simon E. Lee

Out of the Dark